P9-DMZ-584

658.872 THO
Thomas, David B.,
The executive's guide to
enterprise social media
strategy : how social
networks are radically

# The Executive's Guide to Enterprise Social Media Strategy

# Wiley & SAS Business Series

The Wiley & SAS Business Series presents books that help senior-level managers with their critical management decisions.

Titles in the Wiley and SAS Business Series include:

*Activity-Based Management for Financial Institutions: Driving Bottom-Line Results* by Brent Bahnub

*Branded! How Retailers Engage Consumers with Social Media and Mobility* by Bernie Brennan and Lori Schafer

*Business Analytics for Managers: Taking Business Intelligence beyond Reporting* by Gert Laursen and Jesper Thorlund

*Business Intelligence Competency Centers: A Team Approach to Maximizing Competitive Advantage* by Gloria J. Miller, Dagmar Brautigam, and Stefanie Gerlach

*Business Intelligence Success Factors: Tools for Aligning Your Business in the Global Economy* by Olivia Parr Rud

*Case Studies in Performance Management: A Guide from the Experts* by Tony C. Adkins

*CIO Best Practices: Enabling Strategic Value with Information Technology, Second Edition* by Joe Stenzel

*Credit Risk Assessment: The New Lending System for Borrowers, Lenders, and Investors* by Clark Abrahams and Mingyuan Zhang

*Credit Risk Scorecards: Developing and Implementing Intelligent Credit Scoring* by Naeem Siddiqi

*Customer Data Integration: Reaching a Single Version of the Truth*, by Jill Dyche and Evan Levy

*Demand-Driven Forecasting: A Structured Approach to Forecasting* by Charles Chase

*Enterprise Risk Management: A Methodology for Achieving Strategic Objectives* by Gregory Monahan

*Executive's Guide to Solvency II* by David Buckham, Jason Wahl, and Stuart Rose

*Fair Lending Compliance: Intelligence and Implications for Credit Risk Management* by Clark R. Abrahams and Mingyuan Zhang

*Information Revolution: Using the Information Evolution Model to Grow Your Business* by Jim Davis, Gloria J. Miller, and Allan Russell

*Manufacturing Best Practices: Optimizing Productivity and Product Quality* by Bobby Hull

*Marketing Automation: Practical Steps to More Effective Direct Marketing* by Jeff LeSueur

*Mastering Organizational Knowledge Flow: How to Make Knowledge Sharing Work* by Frank Leistner

*Performance Management: Finding the Missing Pieces (to Close the Intelligence Gap)* by Gary Cokins

*Performance Management: Integrating Strategy Execution, Methodologies, Risk, and Analytics* by Gary Cokins

*The Business Forecasting Deal: Exposing Bad Practices and Providing Practical Solutions* by Michael Gilliland

*The Data Asset: How Smart Companies Govern Their Data for Business Success* by Tony Fisher

*The New Know: Innovation Powered by Analytics* by Thornton May

*Visual Six Sigma: Making Data Analysis Lean* by Ian Cox, Marie A Gaudard, Philip J. Ramsey, Mia L. Stephens, and Leo Wright

For more information on any of the above titles, please visit www.wiley.com.

# The Executive's Guide to Enterprise Social Media Strategy

*How Social Networks Are Radically Transforming Your Business*

## David B. Thomas

## Mike Barlow

FOUNTAINDALE PUBLIC LIBRARY DISTRICT
300 West Briarcliff Road
Bolingbrook, IL 60440-2894
(630) 759-2102

**WILEY**

John Wiley & Sons, Inc.

Copyright © 2011 by SAS Institute, Inc. All rights reserved.

Published by John Wiley & Sons, Inc., Hoboken, New Jersey.

Published simultaneously in Canada.

No part of this publication may be reproduced, stored in a retrieval system, or transmitted in any form or by any means, electronic, mechanical, photocopying, recording, scanning, or otherwise, except as permitted under Section 107 or 108 of the 1976 United States Copyright Act, without either the prior written permission of the Publisher, or authorization through payment of the appropriate per-copy fee to the Copyright Clearance Center, Inc., 222 Rosewood Drive, Danvers, MA 01923, (978) 750-8400, fax (978) 646-8600, or on the Web at www.copyright.com. Requests to the Publisher for permission should be addressed to the Permissions Department, John Wiley & Sons, Inc., 111 River Street, Hoboken, NJ 07030, (201) 748-6011, fax (201) 748-6008, or online at www.wiley.com/go/permissions.

Limit of Liability/Disclaimer of Warranty: While the publisher and author have used their best efforts in preparing this book, they make no representations or warranties with respect to the accuracy or completeness of the contents of this book and specifically disclaim any implied warranties of merchantability or fitness for a particular purpose. No warranty may be created or extended by sales representatives or written sales materials. The advice and strategies contained herein may not be suitable for your situation. You should consult with a professional where appropriate. Neither the publisher nor author shall be liable for any loss of profit or any other commercial damages, including but not limited to special, incidental, consequential, or other damages.

For general information on our other products and services or for technical support, please contact our Customer Care Department within the United States at (800) 762-2974, outside the United States at (317) 572-3993 or fax (317) 572-4002.

Wiley also publishes its books in a variety of electronic formats. Some content that appears in print may not be available in electronic books. For more information about Wiley products, visit our web site at www.wiley.com.

*Library of Congress Cataloging-in-Publication Data:*

Thomas, David B., 1952-
  The executive's guide to enterprise social media strategy : how social networks are radically transforming your business / David B. Thomas, Mike Barlow.
      p. cm.—(Wiley & SAS business series)
   Includes index.
    ISBN 978-0-470-88602-1 (hardback); 978-1-118-00521-7 (ebk); 978-1-118-00522-4 (ebk); 978-1-118-00523-1 (ebk)
    1. Business enterprises–Computer networks.   2. Strategic planning–Computer networks.   3. Social media–Economic aspects.   4. Online social networks–Economic aspects.   I. Barlow, Mike.   II. Title.
   HD30.37.T49 2011
   006.7068'4–dc22

                                                    2010037966

Printed in the United States of America

10  9  8  7  6  5  4  3  2  1

*For Jean and Conrad (a.k.a. The Mrs. and The Boy)*
*and*
*For Darlene, Janine, and Paul*

# Contents

# Foreword

Frankly, this book is too fun to cover anything to do with the enterprise.

You're never going to convince anyone in your company that this book is worthwhile, because it's actually useful, and it's interesting, and much more than this, it's engaging and funny (I mean, snicker and blurt out a little laugh funny), and as I once racked up over 16 years in the enterprise telecommunications world, I know that funny and engaging are illegal inside companies.

How are you ever going to convince an executive that learning from other people at other enterprise companies who successfully implemented social media tools into their workplace is worth anything? By interviewing people inside and outside the gray cubicle nation, Dave Thomas and Mike Barlow are ruining anyone's chance of thinking this book was just concocted out of nothing one day while waiting for their laundry to dry.

I don't know Mike Barlow very well. I'm sure he's nice, or at least types fast, because otherwise, why would you write a book with him? But I know Dave Thomas—sorry, David B. Thomas. I met him while he was working for America's "Best Company to Work For" (well, that's what *Fortune* said), which was a big enterprise company, where Dave brought enterprise social media into its fold. Because I don't know anything about Mike personally, I'll just say that he invented dolphins. Yes. That's right.

I have a burning passion for enterprise culture, or, rather, whenever I visit an enterprise, I get the terrible and irresistible urge to change most enterprise cultures, because I feel like the front door was a time machine, in some aspects, and I just want to help them understand that the world outside has changed since the days of President Reagan. This book, such as it is, is a time machine set to forward, set to next.

In all seriousness, the book does what I'm doing here: It coats lots of really important subjects and lots of actionable advice in a little bit of humor, a little bit of well-turned phrase, and actually manages the impressive duty of keeping one's eyes open all the way to the end.

This is to say, it's NOT LIKE OTHER BOOKS ABOUT ENTERPRISE PROCESSES, CULTURE, AND TECHNOLOGY.

So, go ahead. Try to get this one explained away on your expense report. Oh wait. You're not allowed an expense report anymore. It's the future. You have to buy things out of your own pocket and hope that no one else in the building steals this book, because it's that good.

The worst part of all this is that if you've smirked even once while reading the foreword, you're probably more like Dave and Mike than you know. You're at least a little bit like me (except maybe you don't take your coffee black and maybe you don't have a bunch of Batman action figures on your bookshelf thingy). And you might actually value what Thomas and Barlow (doesn't that make them sound like private eyes?) have written.

I'm giving this book a bad review, for having 100 fewer pages than most books I'm forced to read. In fact, I'm going to pan it when it comes out in the mainstream, because, frankly, only people who want their enterprise to succeed will read it anyway, and they don't care what reviews say. They run in search of facts and details and useful, actionable information.

In fact, maybe this book is like *Fight Club*. Let's not talk about it. Let's keep it to ourselves and appear BRILLIANT to the bosses. You with me? Say nothing.

Shhhh.

Chris Brogan, *New York Times* bestselling coauthor
of *Trust Agents*, and publisher of chrisbrogan.com

# Preface

When this book was initially conceived, social media was still considered a relatively new phenomenon, and the main purpose of the book was to address the sense of skepticism expressed by many top executives about the value of social media in enterprise-level business environments.

In the few months between this initial conception and the launch of the book project, the notion that social media was some kind of trend or fad had pretty much vanished. It was replaced by a more palpable sense of awareness that social media was growing and evolving so rapidly that only a fool would purposely ignore it.

This heightened sense of astonishment pushed the book in a different direction, and the finished text you are reading reflects this shift in emphasis. The original book would have started at the 40,000-foot level and stayed there for the duration. This version of the book offers a much broader and more immediately practical view of the current state of corporate social media. Most important, it includes actionable advice that can be put to use by any company, right now.

*The Executive's Guide to Enterprise Social Media Strategy* is composed of three parts: Part I is a high-level strategic overview of the impact of newer social collaborative technologies on society, culture, and business. It serves as a prelude and a foundation for Parts II and III, which dive into the nitty-gritty tactical details of developing and managing successful corporate social media strategies. Parts II and III include summaries titled "What You Can Do Right Now" to help you get started and focus on the tactics that will have immediate value.

All three parts of the book are entertaining, useful, and intentionally provocative. Part I was written primarily by Mike Barlow, a business journalist and management consultant. Parts II and III were written primarily by David B. Thomas, drawing on the nearly two years he spent developing social media strategy, policy, and training as social media manager at SAS. In creating the content for this book, both authors have drawn extensively from their own personal experiences and from stories, anecdotes, and information culled from numerous in-depth interviews conducted with various expert sources.

# Acknowledgments

## DAVE

Almost every name you read in this book represents someone who went out of his or her way to talk to us and share what's working. One of the beautiful things about social media, at least here in late-2010, is how open and honest the practitioners are about what they're doing. The people helping to bring this revolution to the corporate world are doing it not just because they see a way to increase their profits but because they know that promoting a more open and honest philosophy and methodology of business communication can truly help make this a better world.

My thanks to all of them who shared so freely of their knowledge and ideas, including Lee Aase, John Bastone, LaSandra Brill, Jeff Cohen, Len Devanna, Bert Dumars, Craig Duncan, Jeanette Gibson, Nathan Gilliatt, Becky Graebe, Allison Green, Annette Green, Patty Hager, Shel Holtz, Nichole Kelly, Charlene Li, Chris Moody, Jeremiah Owyang, Katie Paine, Christopher S. Penn, Kirsten Watson, and Zena Weist.

Thanks to my SAS boss, Kelly LeVoyer, for her support and encouragement, and to the folks in my chain of command there who saw the value of this book, including SAS External Communications Director Pamela Meek and CMO (and blogger) Jim Davis.

My SAS colleague John Balla deserves a huge round of applause and maybe a big bottle of fancy olive oil for his help with the *Social Media Cookbook for Marketing*, some of which ended up in this book. John and his colleagues, ably led by Deb Orton, demonstrate every day the perfect combination of level-headedness combined with a spirit of creativity and adventure that business folks need to make this stuff work.

Alison Bolen of SAS deserves a special mention as well. Even before I came to work there, she was showing people the value of these new communications channels. Working with her to bring these tools and techniques to fruition has been a joy. She has been an invaluable ally and sounding board (as well as a patient ear at those times when it wasn't such a joy).

I'd like to thank my friend and writing partner Mike Barlow for bringing me in to what was already a greenlighted book project with a great publisher like Wiley already on board. What more could a new author ask for (other than more hours in the day)? Mike taught me everything I know about writing a book. So if there's anything here you don't like, please take it up with him.

And finally, I'd like to thank my dad, David Thomas, career marketer and business leader, blogger, and author of *The Common Sense Manager*, for providing me with a lifelong example of how to be passionate about your work and the value of sharing that passion with others.

## MIKE

From my perspective, this book is largely a work of journalism. As a result, I am indebted to my sources for sharing their time, knowledge, and wisdom so generously.

I could not have written my parts of the book without the active cooperation and participation of John Bastone, Steven Bailey, Matthew Chamberlin, Kendall Collins, Ginger Conlon, Kelly Feller, Christopher Gatewood, Paul Greenberg, Jamie Grenney, Winnie Ko, Brent Leary, Eugene Lee, Liza Emin Levitt, Christopher Lynch, Britton Manasco, Pem McNerney, Hunter Muller, Jeanne Murray, Viviana Padilla, Mark Polansky, Laurie Ruettimann, Brad Samargya, Jeffrey Schick, David Meerman Scott, Euan Semple, Ruth Stevens, Luis Suarez, Lucas Swineford, Teka Thomas, Pamela Warren, and Sean Whiteley.

I owe special thanks to Don Peppers for recommending several terrific books, including *The Wealth of Networks* and *The Rational Optimist*.

Don also planted several ideas in my mind that took root and blossomed during the writing of this book. For those ideas, and for the time that Don spent chatting with me on the phone, I am truly grateful.

I would also like to thank my mom, Edith G. Barlow, who remains the best copy editor I know.

# Introduction

*There are some enterprises in which a careful disorderliness is the true method.*

—Herman Melville

First, let's define some terms. Sharing a common understanding of these terms will help all of us dodge some of the confusion lurking around the subject of this book. These definitions are vast oversimplifications, but no matter. They will get us started on our journey, more or less together.

**Social networking:** Humans sharing knowledge with other humans outside of their immediate pair-bond families.

**Social computing:** Systems of hardware, software, and firmware that enable social networking in a digital environment.

**Social media:** Platforms specifically designed to make social computing available to anyone with a device capable of connecting to the Internet.

**Enterprise 2.0:** A term coined by Andrew McAfee, a professor at the Harvard School of Business, to describe the impact of social networking, social computing, and social media on business organizations.

OK, now we can begin. Clearly, you've already heard a lot about social media and you're wondering how it can help your business or help your career. That's probably why you're reading this book, right? Our goal is to take some of the mystery out of social media. After all, it's just another tool.

Or is it? Saying that social media is just another tool is a little bit like saying the telephone is just another tool or the Internet is just another tool. OK, maybe you're right. They are all tools. But from that perspective, fire is just a tool. The wheel? Just another tool . . .

Well, hold on to your hat. At first glance, *every* new invention looks like just another handy tool. But isn't it funny how some inventions wind up changing the world? The light bulb. The atomic bomb. The disposable razor. The birth control pill.

## COUNTRY VILLAGE OR GLEAMING CITY?

Euan Semple speaks frequently about social media to corporate audiences. Based in the United Kingdom, he was director of knowledge management at the BBC, where he helped developed the BBC's first social networking tools. He has since served as a social media consultant to major organizations such as Nokia, the World Bank, and NATO (the North Atlantic Treaty Organization).

Euan sees social media as more of an enabling technology than a driving force. The distinction between enabler and driver is important, because it underscores what seems to be the inevitability of social media emerging as a common, worldwide platform. Here's what Euan told us in a recent conversation via Skype:

> As is the case so often, it's not so much the technology
> that's driving the changes—it's that the technology has
> come along at a time when things were changing anyway.
>
> The implicit or explicit contract between individuals of
> the organizations they work for has changed over the last
> decade or so. The old promise of stability and safety in
> return for allegiance has fallen apart. The days when you
> had a job for life are gone.
>
> As a result, more and more people are aware of
> their need to build up their own capabilities and their

own networks and start looking after themselves, if you like.

Euan paints a picture of a world that is very different from the one described in most textbooks on corporate management. In this world, social media isn't just an emerging and potentially very useful business tool; it's the salient feature of an evolutionary—or perhaps *de*evolutionary—trend in which people are rediscovering their personal economic fragility and, as a result, gaining new perspectives on their responsibility for shaping their own destinies.

At the same time, corporations are rediscovering the intrinsic business value of their "humanness" and are making room for practices that encourage more participation and more engagement from their employees and their customers. "I think we're trying to get back something that we've lost over the past 30 or 40 years," says Euan.

From the Industrial Revolution until very recently, business has been all about "tidying and linking and categorizing things" into big chunks that appear manageable. But there's a price for this illusion of manageability and control, says Euan.

> I'm more and more convinced that we're actually losing a lot in the process. Very often, the interesting bits happen in the cracks between the big chunks—in the unpredictable, in the unlabeled, in the unexpected, in the messiness.
>
> The willingness to embrace that messiness, to work with that messiness and to make it effective, is really important.
>
> I'll often use the analogy of old villages that grow up haphazardly. There's no predetermined architectural style, there's no uniform color to their roofs. They've got windy paths and lots of human-scale architecture.
>
> People can relate to these old villages. People feel comfortable in them. They know where the church is and where the pub is. There are these well-worn paths that people feel comfortable using. And people feel comfortable standing on street corners talking to each other.

Modern cities, however, can be cold, large, unfriendly, and ultimately confusing. "The scale of the buildings is inhuman. Each street looks much like the previous street. You don't feel like hanging around and chatting," says Euan.

One of the lessons he learned when starting up the BBC's social media program was to keep it simple and let it grow organically—much like those old villages. Having too many rules—or setting expectations too high—can frighten people away from social media programs.

> You don't want to coerce people into using social
> media. You can't force people to blog. You need to
> entice them into participating by offering something
> that's attractive and interesting.

Patience is the key virtue when introducing a social media program, he says. "Whatever you're trying to accomplish with social media will happen one person at a time, and for their reasons, not yours."

Corporations themselves face a choice, he says. They can model themselves to resemble old country villages or new cities. With social media, perhaps they can have both: the gleaming efficiency of the modern metropolis and the comforting messiness—and humanity—of the country village.

## BEYOND DISRUPTIVE

There's no question that social media is a game-changer. It touches and transforms so many aspects of our lives that we've already lost count. Calling it "disruptive" somehow feels like an understatement. For the moment, let's focus on what social media is—and how it can help make our businesses more efficient, more effective, more customer-friendly, and more profitable.

We recently caught up with marketing expert David Meerman Scott, whose bestselling book, *The New Rules of Marketing & PR*, is considered the gold standard for practical advice about social media. David believes that social media is already revolutionizing business communications. Here's a snippet of our conversation with him:

> We're going through a revolution in the way people
> communicate. I think it's the most significant revolution
> in communications since the invention of the printing
> press.

> It's so critically important to understand what's happening right now. This revolution will be transformational for all kinds of businesses—big and small, private and public, B-to-B and B-to-C. It will be transformational for non-profits and government agencies too.

> Organizations that don't understand the consequences of this revolution will be left in the dust. They will miss opportunities and they will leave themselves open to new dangers.

David also notes that social media is eliminating the need for many of the physical meetings that tend to occupy large portions of the typical workday.

> In the old days, you went to work in the morning and you stayed until the evening. Everything happened in the office or at meetings you attended. Very little work got done after 6 p.m. or on weekends or on holidays.

The first generation of home offices and "virtual workspaces" didn't offer much in the way of improvement. They were physically similar to traditional offices—you sat at a desk in front of a computer, tethered to your telephone and your fax machine.

Today, thanks to a growing variety of collaborative social technologies, people can work virtually from anywhere, at any time. "It doesn't really matter anymore where you are," says David.

Social media, he says, "allows us to compress time." It gives us the power to decide when we want to join a conversation. So instead of being locked into back-to-back meetings, we can contribute meaningfully to dozens of online "meetings"—without offending or displeasing anyone.

The ability to "time shift" our work, much in the same way that we "time-shift" TV programs with our digital video recorders, represents a fundamental change in our approach to doing business. As David says, "the manifestations of time and space go away."

It's almost too good to be true: The everyday cost of doing business drops, and productivity goes up. Are we dreaming?

Nope, it's real. Social media is revolutionizing the way we do business—and the revolution has only begun to get started!

You don't have to be an economist to see the advantages of digitally enabled social networking in a business environment. And you don't need to be an especially visionary leader to see why your business needs a social networking strategy. It seems pretty clear that social media is a productivity engine. In the same way that PCs changed the way office work is performed, social computing is changing the way *all* work is performed.

## STEP ASIDE, FRED TAYLOR . . .

Social media, it seems, is about to stand Frederick Winslow Taylor on his head. Taylor, as you know, was the father of scientific management, and his quest for efficiency was legendary. He believed that the key to productivity was standardization. Under Taylor, jobs were broken down into tasks that could be precisely timed and measured. Inefficient practices were rooted out and abolished. Woe to the worker who brought his or her own sense of individual purpose—or, worse yet, creativity—to the assembly line.

To be fair, there are some sectors of the economy—such as manufacturing—in which Taylor's methods still make sense. But as manufacturing becomes more automated, and as the rest of the global economy shifts more and more toward services, Taylor's relentless focus on worker efficiency is beginning to look a bit old hat.

Until someone figures out a way to automate creativity, we're going to need workers who can think fast and respond appropriately to increasingly complex challenges posed by increasingly complex markets. The best way to make these kinds of workers productive is by giving them a platform that supports and amplifies their natural human creativity. That platform is social media.

## SOCIAL MEDIA OR WHAT?

When we began conducting interviews for this book, one of the first questions our interview subjects would ask was "Is this book about social media or enterprise 2.0?" or words to that general effect. Our standard answer was "Both!"

After a couple of interviews, however, we realized that what people were really asking us was "Is this another book about Facebook, LinkedIn, Twitter, and YouTube?"

For most people, Facebook, LinkedIn, Twitter, YouTube, and all of their various digital cousins represent the "social" face of social media. So our typical response was to say something like "No, we're writing a book about the business uses of social media."

Unfortunately, that response would usually elicit a reply that went something like this:

> Oh, you mean like how Disney Pixar has a Buzz Lightyear page on Facebook to promote *Toy Story 3* and Lady Gaga has a MySpace page for *The Fame Monster* where you can download "Telephone?"

And then we would say something along these lines:

> No, actually we're writing a book about how some companies are using social media to promote and support collaboration, teamwork, and communication across the modern extended enterprise, which includes stakeholders and partners within and without the traditional corporate boundaries.

> And we're also looking at how really smart companies use social media to generate leads, identify prospects, improve customer lifetime value, and drive down marketing costs.

Then the person we're interviewing usually says, "Oh, that's what I was hoping you'd say," or words to that effect, and the interview begins in earnest.

## WHY NOW?

If the hype around social media seems particularly breathless and frenetic, it's because most of the experts, pundits, and hypesters (pronounced *hype*-sters, like *hip*sters or *ham*sters) who are talking, writing, and blogging about social media are actually way behind the curve when it comes to understanding the technologies driving its widespread adoption.

Here's what you have to know about social media so you can fully understand why it's not about to just go away or vanish or be replaced by another cool trend.

The reason social media is expanding so quickly is partially accidental. Yes, social media is another of those pesky worldwide phenomena, like influenza, that ride the tricky roller coaster of fortune. It's always difficult to step back and say, "Wow, that's pretty random," especially when it's something affecting your business, but there it is. Luck plays a role, and there's no point in denying it.

The reason social media looks more like a tsunami than a trend is that, like a tsunami, the real action is taking place beneath the surface.

You can ask yourself, "Which came first, the chicken or the egg?" all day long, but it seems pretty obvious that social media got its biggest boost from broadband and that it will get an even bigger boost from wireless. When cloud computing really kicks into high gear, social media will get another huge lift.

Social media lives in the global information technology (IT) infrastructure and travels across the global communications infrastructure. So it makes sense that the faster and more powerful those infrastructures become, the faster and more powerful social media will become.

A few years ago, it seemed as if everyone were talking about the "convergence" of telephone, cable, and Internet service. That convergence was made possible by huge investments in new infrastructure by the telecoms and cable providers. Today, we enjoy the fruits of that labor, even as we curse the monthly costs.

A similar convergence is driving social media. As companies invest more heavily in advanced mobile computing and cloud computing technologies, social media will get what amounts to a free ride.

If you're a history buff, all of this should evoke thoughts of the influenza pandemic of 1920 and its aftermath. What's genuinely fascinating and unique about social media, however, is that it's self-propagating. It's the medium *and* the message, rolled into one handy bundle. Where's Marshall McLuhan when we really need him?

## SO, WHAT'S THE BEST WAY TO SKIN A MASTODON?

Social networking is not a new phenomenon. It's been a part of human culture for the past two million years, give or take a few dozen millennia. When our ancestors started organizing themselves into social groups of hunters and gatherers, they also began communicating and sharing information with each other.

Although there isn't much evidence to suggest that these early humans developed more than a rudimentary kit of tools, the fossil records show a surge of creativity about 40,000 years ago, in what archeologists call the Upper Paleolithic Period.

Suddenly, people were using specialized tools and working together to perform increasingly complex tasks, such as hunting, trapping, killing, butchering, cooking, and consuming large prey. This isn't a minor detail in the evolutionary history of humankind; it's the killing and eating of large prey—big animals that are chock full of protein and fat—that gives humans the edge over any potential competitors.

The hunter-gatherer clans of the Upper Paleolithic Period functioned as real teams. Members of the clan communicated with each other, shared knowledge, and collaborated to produce results that far outstripped the accomplishments of other primates. Within these primitive "corporations," critical knowledge was transferred socially, from one person to the next—there weren't any other mechanisms available.

About 10,000 years ago, humans developed agriculture. Over the next several thousand years, clans and tribes were gradually replaced by villages, towns, cities, and eventually nations. It took a lot of knowledge to sustain a growing civilization, but somehow our early relatives figured out how to pass the knowledge around and keep it from getting lost.

Again, the primary mode of transmission was social—one person telling something to someone else. Of course, if you had a loud voice, you could pass your knowledge along to several people at once. And yes, writing enabled some people to capture knowledge and store it on various media (stone, clay, papyrus, vellum, parchment, etc.), but unless you knew how to read—and few people did—you couldn't access that knowledge.

Everything changed with Johannes Gutenberg's invention of the printing press and movable type in the middle of the fifteenth century. Suddenly it was possible to share knowledge widely. There had been a pent-up demand for knowledge during the Middle Ages; Gutenberg's press set off a revolution that fed on that repressed demand. The

Renaissance, the Reformation, and the Enlightenment all swiftly followed.

The accelerating pace of innovation and progress began to resemble a natural force, a fierce storm sweeping aside all vestiges of the past. The nineteenth century brought the telegraph, the telephone, and the radio; the twentieth century brought television, computers, the Internet, and the World Wide Web.

And now, at the beginning of the second decade of the twenty-first century, we contemplate the emergence of the newest branch of Gutenberg's expanding revolution: social computing.

Social computing brings social networking—an activity that began in the Stone Age—into the here and now. Fortunately for all of us, the timing could not be more perfect.

## QUESTIONS YOU SHOULD BE PREPARED TO ANSWER

OK, maybe you're wondering whether it would really be a good idea to include a slide of early humans hunting down a mastodon when you're trying to justify more spending on social media. Fair enough. Let's focus instead for a moment on the most pressing and most relevant questions you are likely to face from skeptical internal audiences. (Don't worry, the answers follow!)

Q. Why does our company need a social media strategy?

A. Because our competitors already have one, and if they don't, they will very soon. Also, many of our current employees— and virtually *all* of our future employees—expect us to develop and support some sort of corporate social media platform.

Q. How do other companies leverage social media to achieve business objectives?

A. In various ways, but mostly by focusing on activities such as lead generation, customer relationship management, public relations, reputation management, knowledge management, internal collaboration, product development, customer service, internal communications, training, and talent management.

Q. How can our company leverage social media to achieve real business goals?

A. Business goals are achieved through the coordination of business processes, so the first step is figuring out which processes can be enhanced or improved by adding social media components. Then the next step is developing social media programs for those processes.

Q. How can our company measure the success of our social media initiatives?

A. There are numerous tools available for measuring the impact of social media programs and initiatives. Many of them are free!

Q. Can social media get us into trouble? What are the best ways for our company to mitigate the risks?

A. There are risks associated with all business activities. Smart companies make sure that representatives from legal, human resources (HR), finance, and risk management are involved in the development of media programs.

Q. Have "best practices" emerged for corporate social media strategies?

A. Yes, but practices vary far and wide. Smart companies make sure that the interests of key functional areas—such as HR, legal, risk, finance, sales, marketing, customer service, and corporate communications—are represented when social media strategies are planned or discussed. Smart companies also make certain that social media strategies are promulgated, explained, and supported across all the functional areas of the organization and that training and incentives are provided to ensure compliance.

Q. Will our company need to hire people with special skills to manage corporate social media initiatives?

A. Special skills are definitely required, but there are probably many people in your organization who already have the skills necessary to manage social media programs. Before putting out the help-wanted sign, find people in the organization with the right skills and assign them to positions on the social media team.

Q. Will social media replace email as the primary platform for business conversations?

A. Probably not soon, although it will likely reduce email traffic considerably.

## CRITICAL AREAS FOR SUCCESS

Although this book is written as a general guide for senior managers and executives, it will also cover crucial topics such as the basic value proposition of social media, metrics, costs, return on investment, executive buy-in, critical skills, staffing, training, technology infrastructure, risk management, competitive business benefits (faster penetration into new markets, multichannel interactions with global customer base, aggregated customer insights through analysis of unstructured data, continuous real-time product feedback, earned media, etc.) and the long-term implications of "getting it wrong."

Here are quick "snapshots" of key areas where social media is already having an impact on your business:

**Sales, Marketing, and Customer Service.** Customer-facing areas of the enterprise such as sales, marketing, and customer service have the most to gain immediately from well-coordinated social media initiatives and programs.

**Human Resources and Talent Management.** Finding, attracting, and retaining high-quality performers will require a dedicated social media strategy for engaging with top talent on a continuous basis and managing complex, multidimensional work/play/family relationships. Since social media is the only platform with the capabilities to manage such relationships effectively and efficiently, HR must transform itself into a social media activity.

**Training and Knowledge Management.** In a turbulent global economy, the only constant is change. Dealing with continuous change requires continual training and extremely efficient systems for sharing business-critical knowledge. Social media is the logical platform for delivering the type of continuous training and learning that rapidly evolving markets demand. This is an area in which social media can have an immediate and positive impact on the corporation, with minimal investment in new infrastructure.

**Internal and External Communications.** Within a very brief span of time, social media will replace traditional channels and platforms used for conveying critical business messaging, both inside and outside the traditional limits of the enterprise. This rapid evolution will dramatically alter the nature of relationships inside and outside the enterprise, creating new stresses and placing additional demands on staff devoted to managing communications. The good news is that social media makes it easier to communicate important information quickly—but that's also the bad news, since it will be harder to police the flow of information across the enterprise and beyond its boundaries.

**Infrastructure and Systems.** Apart from issues raised by the increased use of social media apps designed for smartphones and other mobile devices, enterprise social media programs should pose relatively few problems from a purely technological perspective. But the very simplicity of social media technology will create a host of new challenges for management. Most of these challenges can be addressed with written guidelines, training, and management sign-off procedures. Other challenges, however, will require new IT systems to monitor and prevent unauthorized use of social media platforms. Additionally, the organization will have to invest in new analytic software to extract valuable information and insight from the huge amounts of unstructured data generated by social media content. This will be the most significant technology challenge, and potentially the most difficult to overcome.

**Governance, Measurement, and Risk Management.** Like any enterprise-wide strategic initiative, social media will require a governing body to ensure compliance with rules and regulations, and alignment with company strategy. Senior management should set up a social media governing board made up of representatives from various units of the enterprise to guarantee that many voices are heard when social media policies are debated and developed. At the same time, a special board within IT or finance should be established to monitor, measure, and report on the progress of social media initiatives. It is also critical to involve representatives from legal and finance in a formal risk management process designed to avoid creating liabilities through inadvertent misuse of information or intellectual capital generated from social media activities.

The net takeaway: In order to be effective components of corporate strategy, social media programs should be developed within a strategic context that ensures alignment with real business goals and objectives. This requires buy-in and cooperation from top management. Failure to obtain consensus at top executive levels of the organization will result in ad hoc, uncoordinated grassroots efforts that produce few tangible benefits.

A final observation before launching headlong into the book: It is not a coincidence that social media is gaining ground as other social, political, and economic systems seem to be withering. Social media is not a symptom of a world gone wrong—it's a collective, cultural response to the failure of systems that were supposed to keep us together, keep us safe, and keep us healthy.

We firmly believe that social media is a global response to various pressures and strains resulting from the emergence of a new global culture. If that's the case, social media is more like an earthquake—an undeniable reminder of immense forces beyond our control.

# PART

## I

---

# The Grand Scheme of Things

It's a sure bet that when people saw the first stone ax, the first bronze spear tip, or the first iron stirrup, someone shook his head sadly, turned to the person next to him, and said, "These kids today with their toys. It's just a fad, the newest thing. It won't last."

As you know, some folks are making similar pronouncements over social media and social networking. Like their ancient skeptical cousins, they are also wrong. Social media and social networking are not symptoms; they are manifestations of the newest era of human evolution. Don't expect them to go away and don't waste time trying to deny their importance. Instead, figure out how to use them to grow your business, reduce your costs, and improve your margins.

# CHAPTER 1

# Speed, Scope, Complexity, Power, and Potential

*What's really going on in technology is not a "social media" revolution but an "e-social" revolution, one that involves not just how we interact with others, but how we choose to create things of value, how we transfer value from soul to soul, how we evaluate our existence and try to improve it.*

—Don Peppers

Here is a great story told to us while we were researching this book. We've taken out the names of the hotels to avoid any appearance of favoritism or bias.

> I'm standing in the queue at Hotel A in Las Vegas, waiting to check in. Normally the check-in queues there move pretty fast, but today they aren't. A bunch of us

are just standing there, waiting with our bags. Something
is clearly wrong at the check-in counter, but no one is
telling us anything. I check Twitter on my iPhone and I
can see that people are tweeting from the queue I'm
standing in. I've experienced this before, and it's
amusing, but no big deal.

Then I see a tweet from someone at the Hotel Z, a couple
of blocks down the Strip. The tweet says something like
"Hey, if you're tired of standing on line at Hotel A, come
on over to Hotel Z. We'll set you up with a room—at 50
percent off the regular price."

Then I see a couple of people pick up their bags and head
out for the taxi stand. Wow, I thought, somebody at
Hotel Z is on the ball.

We're including this story because it's true and because in one fell
swoop it illustrates the speed, scope, complexity, power, and potential
of social media. And most important from our perspective, it high-
lights the principal point of this book: You need a strategy for dealing
with the social media phenomenon.

Let's take a closer look at the scenario described by our source in
the queue. It's an interesting story, but what makes it especially relevant to this book? Can you guess?

What makes it relevant is that Hotel Z clearly had a strategy for
generating revenue from its social media resources. The management
team at Hotel Z wasn't just using social media because social media is
cool—it was using social media to make money!

At some point, the management team at Hotel Z said, "OK, we'll
invest in social media—but only because we expect a return on our
investment within a reasonable period of time." Then the management team delegated someone to be in charge of social media and
charged that person with developing a set of operating guidelines,
devising an operating plan, and executing on the plan. There was a
budget (for some training, some apps, and some additional staff hours)
and a target (something to aim for).

The people assigned to the hotel's social media initiative understood clearly that at the end of the day their primary objective was
acquiring new customers—fresh revenue—for the hotel.

Maybe at some point down the road, the hotel's social media program might also include some customer retention activities, some customer relationship management activities, and some pure marketing or promotional activities. All of that would be cool. But what we like about the hotel's initial approach to social media was that it focused on achieving a very tangible, highly measurable result—new revenue.

Here's another quick story, told to us by Kendall Collins, the chief marketing officer at salesforce.com.

> Jim Steele, our chief customer officer and president of worldwide sales, was in London, meeting with the CEO of a large software company that uses our products. When Jim updated his status on Chatter (our enterprise social collaboration application and platform), he mentioned the meeting. While Jim is meeting with the CEO in London, somebody deep in our accounting department back in San Francisco reads Jim's update and a light goes on in his head. It turns out the CEO's company is late on its account payable. The accountant posts an update on Chatter, and Jim shows it to the CEO. The CEO says, "Oh, my God!" and sends a message to his accounts payable department. They wired us the money that same day!

Keep these stories in mind as you read the rest of this book.

## THEY LAUGHED AT THE WRIGHT BROTHERS

In the early years of the twentieth century, automobiles and airplanes were ridiculed as overly complex contraptions with little commercial value. In the early years of the twenty-first century, social media was regarded with similarly low esteem. Social media was derided as an unintended consequence of the Internet. It was largely dismissed as a time waster, something used mostly by kids to exchange schoolyard gossip and photos of friends at parties.

Few people laugh at social media today. In Iraq and Afghanistan, it is used by U.S. Army officers to exchange lifesaving tactical information. In Iran, it is used by opponents of the government to organize rallies. In the commercial sphere, it is used by companies to promote brands, attract attention to new products, and collect valuable insight from customers.

According to comScore, the Internet marketing research company, social media networking accounts for 11 percent of all time spent online in the United States, making it one of the most popular activities across the Web. One study reports that 96 percent of Gen Y has already joined at least one online social network, while another study claims that social media has overtaken porn as the most popular activity on the Internet.

As one popular blogger put it recently, "If Facebook were a country it would be the world's 4th largest between the United States and Indonesia."

That extraordinarily high level of acceptance makes it foolhardy for businesses to ignore or downplay the economic value of social media as a comprehensive platform for external and internal communications.

Some experts believe that social media is poised to replace email as an enterprise solution for facilitating collaboration, teamwork, and knowledge sharing across large organizations. In some contexts, social media has replaced Google as the preferred method of search. At several innovative corporations, social media has already become the preferred platform for disseminating critical business information quickly and effectively.

With amazing speed, social media has emerged as a key component of enterprise strategy at large, decentralized organizations where being "first to market" is a critical competitive advantage. Early adopters have already demonstrated that effective social media programs create competitive advantages—in both developed and emerging markets.

Some corporations have already put enterprise social media into the "pockets" of their employees by using readily available social media apps designed for the newest generation of smartphones and mobile devices. These innovative uses of newer social media technologies will completely revolutionize crucial business functions such as sales, marketing, and customer support, where rapid access to expert information often makes the difference between success and failure.

## A WORLD OF NEW CHALLENGES AND OPPORTUNITIES

The rapid acceptance of social media as a business solution presents an array of new challenges and opportunities for management. Executives are spending more time responding to questions about how they plan to leverage social media technologies to achieve strategic business objectives. They are also spending more time considering spending requests for a multitude of new social media projects. These requests are boiling up from all parts of the enterprise.

In effect, these demands will echo the demands for high-speed voice and data networks that boiled up after people began using their laptops and mobile phones for work. Today, high-speed connectivity is a given. Tomorrow, social media will seem just as ordinary. But getting to that state of ordinariness will require imagination, innovation, thought leadership, planning, and successful execution.

## GETTING A FIRM GRASP ON A VIRAL PHENOMENON

Like many new technologies, social media entered the corporate landscape at the grassroots level and is growing virally. As a result, executive-level awareness and oversight of social media has been ad hoc, informal, and haphazard.

This situation must change, and it must change rapidly. Social media is not going away, it's getting bigger. Yet despite all that has been written and said about social media, it remains a mystery for top management. Most executives still regard social media as a *social* phenomenon and have not yet grasped its importance as a *business* tool.

Enterprise social media strategy is the logical response to a worldwide trend that offers enormous potential—and poses enormous risks—for competitive organizations.

Companies that develop comprehensive enterprise social media strategies will gain competitive advantages in swiftly moving markets. They are also likely to avoid the risks associated with social media activities.

Top management should take responsibility for making enterprise social media strategy development a priority and devote sufficient resources toward ensuring that social media programs are developed, rolled out, managed, and measured in ways that support the stated business goals and objectives of the enterprise.

## WHAT'S THE HURRY?

*Why now? What's the hurry? Can it wait?*

Those are all perfectly valid questions for busy executives to ask when confronting the need for developing a corporate social media strategy.

Here are three quick answers:

1. Your employees have Facebook and Twitter accounts. They watch videos on YouTube. They are already living in a social media universe. *That* is their reality. Your business needs a strategy for operating in that universe.

2. Remember when everyone started using wireless phones and you wondered how long it would be before your company needed a wireless strategy? Social media poses a similar challenge. Like wireless, it's a grassroots phenomenon that infiltrates your business and changes the way people behave. You need a strategy for dealing with it.

3. Your competitors are already using social media. Yes, they are.

## TOO NEWFANGLED FOR YOU?

One executive told us point blank that his company would not "start messing around with social media because we never use bleeding-edge technologies. We only use stable technologies."

We're sorry to disappoint any readers who were looking for cheap techno-thrills in this book. Social media apps do not require bleeding-edge or even cutting-edge technologies. Virtually all of the technology required to support a comprehensive social media strategy is already mature technology.

We're sure that you are familiar with the Technology Adoption Life Cycle chart made famous in *Crossing the Chasm* by Geoffrey Moore. It looks like a bell curve, with "innovators" at the beginning of the timeline and "laggards" at the end. By now, any business that isn't using social media is a laggard. It is behind the curve. Is that ever a good place for a business to be?

Look at it this way: Your mom and your grandma probably use social media to share family photos. If you have a smartphone, you probably use social media to check out new restaurants and find cheap parking spots downtown. Most teens that we know don't just use social media—they consume it. In fact, it's not really a stretch to suggest that many teens are addicted to social media. But that's the subject for another book.

Like it or not, we already live in a hypersocialized world. So if you haven't developed a sense of urgency about the need for a corporate social media strategy, now's the time. Embrace the challenge; waiting is not a viable option.

## A VERY COOL SCENARIO

Here is the transcript of a hypothetical scenario—a semifictional "pastiche" of tweets, as it were—developed by the nice folks at Socialtext, a Palo Alto–based software vendor to demonstrate the use of social media in a competitive business situation. Eugene Lee, the affable CEO of Socialtext, assured us that the user-generated microblogs in this multitier conversation represent credible approximations of real events.

The main "characters" in the scenario are Ryker Solar, a manufacturer of solar power cells; Van Company, one of Ryker's customers; Joseph Hines, a senior sales exec at Ryker; Mandy Cunningham, a junior sales exec at Ryker; Caroline Decker, a customer service rep in the Ryker's western regional office; Kevin Rice, Ryker's vice president of sales; and several automated software applications, or "bots."

The scenario begins with a short post from a Ryker's TwitterBot, an app that monitors Twitter for mentions of Ryker or its customers.

Twitter Bot *one minute ago* **to Ryker**
<VanCompany> **@RykerSolar** Can you confirm that our order is shipping ontime. If we don't have it by next week it will affect the delivery of our new vehicles.

Joe Hines sees the Twitter bot's message on the company's social media platform and gets worried. He pings the company's CRM bot, an app that interfaces with Ryker's customer database, and receives this reply:

> **CRM Bot** *one minute ago*
> VanCompany - HQ: Palo Alto, Ca. Annual revenue: $52 Million. Customer Representative: Mandy Cunningham

From the CRM bot, Joe sees that Van Company is a big customer. He quickly posts a short message for Mandy.

> **You** *one minute ago*
> Mandy Cunningham There was a tweet from one of your customers, VanCo, that I think you should know about.

Mandy doesn't waste an instant replying—there's a nice commission at stake, and she doesn't want to damage a profitable relationship with a good customer.

> **Mandy Cunningham** *one minute ago*
> Joseph Hines We need to solve this right away. I've been negotiating with VanCo for a new $20 million dollar order for solar refrigerated vans.

Mandy also posts the most recent version of her sales presentation to Van Company.

> **Mandy Cunningham** *one minute ago*
> Mandy Cunningham updated VanCompany Sales Presentation, saying: "Here's the latest update of the sales presentetation I've been working on for them -- we're critical to their next-generation delivery product strategy."
> *Reshared by* Mandy Cunningham *in the VanCompany Account Team group*

But hold on, the situation is getting more complicated. According to the inventory bot, an app that monitors the company's inventory levels, they're running low on a component that's necessary to complete the order. Inventory bot automatically posts an alert to Ryker's Western Region office.

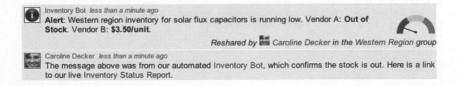

> **Inventory Bot** *less than a minute ago*
> **Alert**: Western region inventory for solar flux capacitors is running low. Vendor A: **Out of Stock**. Vendor B: **$3.50/unit**.
> *Reshared by* Caroline Decker *in the Western Region group*

> **Caroline Decker** *less than a minute ago*
> The message above was from our automated Inventory Bot, which confirms the stock is out. Here is a link to our live Inventory Status Report.

Caroline posts a message for Kevin Rice, Ryker's sales veep.

Caroline Decker  *less than a minute ago*
Kevin Rice, what should we do here? The price from our alternate supplier is above our approved unit cost.

Kevin replies immediately.

Kevin Rice  *less than a minute ago*
The new sale will cover the extra cost. Caroline Decker go ahead and make the order.

Inventory bot monitors the order and posts its own message.

Inventory Bot  *one minute later* to **Ryker**
Order submitted for solar flux capacitors; delivery will arrive within 48 hours.
*Reshared by **@CarolineDecker** in the Western Region group*

[ Track Delivery ]

Everyone can breathe a sigh of relief. Joe posts a quick "thank you" to the team.

Joseph Hines  *one minute later* to **Ryker**
Thanks everyone for working together so quickly to resolve this customer issue.

Twitter bot relays a follow-up tweet from Van Company.

Twitter Bot  *less than a minute ago*  to **Ryker**
<VanCompany> @**RykerSolar** Awesome! Thank you for the speedy response. ☺

CRM bot chimes in . . .

CRM Bot  *less than a minute ago*  to **Ryker**
VanCompany order closes: $20 million.

. . . and Mandy's commission is saved!

Mandy Cunningham  *less than a minute ago*
Thanks to everyone involved!

All of this took place within the span of about 10 minutes. As author David Meerman Scott observed earlier, social media really is compressing time!

The quick resolution of the problem is indeed impressive. But what's even more impressive is the ability of the social media platform to surface critical information from multiple sources—several enterprise business systems, an external social media program, various people in different locations—and present all that information in an easily recognizable format.

Notice that while the initial message that gets the ball rolling is sent over Twitter, which is a very public medium, the rest of the messaging takes place behind Ryker's firewall. The conversations among the members of the Ryker team are essentially private business conversations taking place on a private social media platform.

The platform enables the team to pull information from public and private sources, examine it together, discuss the business implications, deal with an exception (the cost of the solar flux capacitors is higher than normally allowed), and reach a management decision resulting in a profitable deal.

We believe that this type of scenario represents one of the best arguments for the adoption of social technology by competitive business organizations. The elegant combination of information from multiple sources and business systems—all in real time—is what makes this scenario so appealing to champions of enterprise social media.

## STEP UP AND MEET THE MILLENNIAL GENERATION

The book is in no way intended to be a gloomy reminder that we are all getting older. But the truth is that we *are* all getting older and eventually we will be replaced and eclipsed by people who are younger than we are.

That's the way of the world. The "Greatest Generation" is replaced by the Baby Boomers. The Boomers are replaced by Generation X. Gen X is replaced by Gen Y, which will be replaced by the Millennials.

Among these newer generations is a growing tribe of "digital natives"— people who grew up surrounded by digital devices and who are accustomed to being connected with their peers and their friends *all of the time*. To them, interconnectedness isn't a luxury, it's a basic necessity of life. If you take away their connectivity, they start getting very anxious.

Again, this isn't a fad, a phase, or a trend. This is the new reality. Organizations that don't adapt to this new reality simply will not be able to attract the talent necessary to compete successfully, and they will be overtaken by organizations that are more accommodating.

As managers and executives, we are responsible for grooming our replacements. But first we have to recruit, hire, and train the younger men and women who will eventually replace us. Those younger people won't come to work for us in the first place unless we create work environments that make sense to them.

Social media is now an integral part of this process of continuous replacement. So rather than consider social media as something trendy, faddish, hip, or outlandish, think of social media as something more akin to electricity and indoor plumbing.

Social media is quickly becoming a basic staple of our increasingly frenetic modern lives. Our advice is simple: Get used to it. Then figure out how to make it work to your advantage. It will be easier than you think.

## JUST WHAT YOU NEEDED: ANOTHER "CONVERGENCE"

As we've already mentioned, social networking is not a new phenomenon. What makes this particular moment in history so crucial, however, is the swift emergence and rapid convergence of three new technologies: social, mobile, and cloud computing.

This convergence has already developed its own momentum, and it's hard to predict its full impact. If you're looking for a convenient image that sums it up, think of the whirlpool that swallows the *Pequod* at the end of *Moby Dick*. Unlike the vortex that seizes Ahab's ship, however, this new convergence is global. One way or another, we are all getting sucked into the maelstrom.

In a recent exchange of emails with Don Peppers, one of the early visionaries of one-to-one marketing, Don confronted the problem of trying to define social media as if it existed in a vacuum, instead of seeing it as one facet of a broader cultural phenomenon. Here's an excerpt from Don's email message:

> I also think the whole "social media" idea is underestimated by most people. Human beings are naturally social animals—we want to have friends, help our friends, play games, share ideas—and we have always wanted to do this, offline before online.
>
> What's really going on in technology is not a "social media" revolution but an "e-social" revolution, one that involves not just how we interact with others, but how we choose to create things of value, how we transfer value from soul to soul, how we evaluate our existence and try to improve it.
>
> It's a revolution, I think, that dwarfs the Industrial Revolution in its impact on the species. So to me the term "social media" is a trivialization of the idea.

Strong stuff, from a really smart guy whom we admire. And since we're not likely to come up with a response that is truly worthy, let's move on to the next chapter.

CHAPTER **2**

# The New Mode
# of Production

*Without a broadly accepted analytic model to
explain these phenomena, we tend to treat
them as curiosities, perhaps transient fads, of
possible significance in one market segment or
another. We should try instead to see them for
what they are: a new mode of production
emerging in the middle of the most advanced
economies in the world.*

—Yochai Benkler, *The Wealth of Networks*

## SOCIAL MEDIA, TEAMWORK, AND COLLABORATION

The best argument for social media in the workplace is that it is
uniquely suited to enable and elevate one of the key elements of
modern business, the team. "A team remains the most flexible and
the most powerful unit of performance, learning and change in any
organization," write Jon R. Katzenbach and Douglas K. Smith in their
seminal management book, *The Wisdom of Teams*.

   Of the many types of organizational units within a modern business, teams are the most effective for responding quickly to

unpredictable changes in rapidly shifting markets. Rigid, top-down corporate hierarchies are dinosaurs; teams are the small, clever mammals who replaced them.

Team performance, according to Katzenbach and Smith, depends on six basics: small size, complementary skills, common purpose, common performance goals, common approach, and mutual accountability. Katzenbach and Smith also list "openness and communication" as important, but not critical, elements of team discipline.

At the risk of picking a fight with two guys who clearly know what they're talking about, we respectfully suggest that "openness and communication" are just as critical, particularly in today's hypersocialized world.

We can argue about the choice of the word "openness"—maybe "candor," "honesty," or "clarity" would be more appropriate. But as a requirement, pure and simple, the word "communication" speaks for itself: Team members need a platform for communicating, not only with other members of the team but with other individuals and other teams that can provide useful, actionable information at a moment's notice.

In today's crazy markets, success depends on two prime factors: innovation and speed. Social media makes it possible for teams to share critical knowledge, bounce around ideas, and formulate action plans very rapidly and very efficiently.

Moreover, social media makes it possible for other people who are not members of the core team per se to join in the conversation and to make meaningful contributions.

This ability to pick up "random noise" is what distinguishes social media from other communication modalities, and what gives it special value. For example, the most common modes of communication within a team are:

1. Face-to-face
2. Phone
3. Email

The problem with all three is that they are, by virtue of their constraints, exclusionary. In other words, if you weren't invited to attend the meeting, or if you weren't invited to participate in the conference call, or if you weren't on the email distribution list, you are *out of the loop*, and the value of whatever knowledge or insight you might have shared with the team drops effectively to zero.

In the scathing words of legendary consultant Bill French, "Email is where knowledge goes to die." The same insight applies to most telephone conversations and all but a few meetings.

But if the team is using social media as its primary platform for collaboration and communication, the exchange of ideas opens up to a much broader audience. Happy accidents, chance encounters, and serendipitous events are now free to occur. The element of randomness is reintroduced, and a whole new world of unintended consequences unfolds like the petals of a dahlia.

OK, we can hear you saying "But that's exactly what we don't want—everybody butting in with their goofy ideas and just getting in the way." You might have a valid point—if the team in question had decided to share its work on Facebook or MySpace.

But in reality—assuming, of course, that your company has a corporate social media strategy in place—the team is going to share its collaborative efforts on a social media platform that might look an awful lot like Facebook or MySpace but is actually a business-friendly solution surrounded by a corporate firewall or running in a secure cloud environment.

Jeffrey Schick, a vice president in IBM's Social Software Group, likes to tell the story of how a brief message—a "microblog"—that he dashed off while getting off a plane serendipitously created more business for the company. In his microblog, which was actually just an update to his profile on IBM's internal social networking platform, he mentioned that he had arrived in the United Arab Emirates. Some of IBM's sales reps in the Middle East noticed Jeff's update and promptly requested that he attend meetings with several of their clients. Here's the story in Jeff's own succinct words:

> Our sales reps saw that I was in the region, and I
> picked up another half-dozen meetings with clients.
> Two of those meetings turned into multi-million dollar
> opportunities for the company. That would have never
> happened before.

Let's take a close look at what happened when Jeff updated his profile. He created value. Not imaginary or theoretical value. Real value! The kind of value that generates cash, and frankly, that's just about the best and most unambiguous form of value there is.

Jeff's calendar doesn't generate value, except maybe for himself and a close circle of associates who need to know where he is and what's on his schedule. His calendar exists in a program tucked safely behind a thick wall of cybersecurity, accessible only to Jeff and a handful of his colleagues. And that's the way it should be, since his calendar also includes confidential and sensitive information.

But when Jeff updated his corporate social media profile—when he shared just a tiny tidbit of the information that usually sits in his calendar—he created real value. In the two or three moments it took him to type out the update, he generated a pretty impressive ROI.

> I won't give half a million people access to my calendar.
> But I'm happy to type a few words, basically saying
> "Here's where I am and here's what I'm doing today."
> That information becomes searchable across IBM, and
> eventually it creates value for someone or some group
> within the organization.

Now imagine little moments like that happening all over IBM, where 400,000 employees and another 19,000 partners share access to a platform of 11,000 interconnected social communities, all created for the purpose of finding and sharing solutions to the problems large and small that crop up like weeds across an extended global enterprise.

Not *everyone* will be monitoring every conversation and scanning the corporate social media platform for every new morsel of information, for two very good reasons:

1. There just isn't time.

2. In a modern corporate computing environment, every keystroke can be tracked.

At some companies, employees construct "communities of interest" within the corporate social media environment. These communities tend to make it easier for people to focus on the information they really need to achieve their business objectives. Communities, by their nature, can also serve as virtual workspaces with virtual fences and boundaries, preventing or impeding access by unauthorized individuals to some kinds of corporate information.

The moral of Jeff Schick's story is that his small gesture resulted in the creation of significant value to the business. Pardon us for using a series of analogies from the good old days of radio, but it's almost as if the corporate social media platform acted like a microphone, transmitter, receiver, tuner, and amplifier. Jeff's whisper became a shout that was heard only by the people who needed to hear it.

This brings us back to Yochai Benkler. In his amazing book, *The Wealth of Networks*, Benkler envisions a world in which the extremely low cost of "publishing" information on the Internet gives rise to a continuous global conversation that, in turn, creates a whole new culture.

In this new culture, we believe, people would share knowledge more or less freely, motivated by a tacit belief and common understanding that the act of sharing knowledge generates value, while the act of hoarding knowledge destroys value.

## MAPPING SOCIAL MEDIA TO RESULTS

Companies with strong corporate social media strategies encouraging participation and involvement in social media networks are already reaping the benefits of the positive cultural evolution suggested by Benkler.

Accenture, the global management consulting, technology services, and outsourcing company, relies on social media to move critical knowledge and information among its more than 181,000 employees working in 200 cities in 52 countries.

Like many of the people who work at Accenture, Steven Bailey wears several hats. On the operational side, he is director of portal and content applications. On the consulting side, he leads the enterprise search and information architecture practice.

We recently caught up with Steven and he walked us through some examples of how the company's social site provides real value to the business:

I'm sitting on the bus on the way into work. I'm checking my overnight email on my iPhone. I see that someone has sent me an old-fashioned email asking me if I know anyone who can put together a highly specialized RFP (request for proposal) related to enterprise search. I don't personally know anyone in my immediate network who has the expertise or knowledge required to help write this RFP.

But we do have a community of practice for enterprise search on our social site.

So I launch our social site application from my iPhone, I start a conversation, I tag it to the enterprise search community of practice and post a message asking if anyone is available to help with the RFP. I also ask if anyone has any assets that we could reuse to help create an estimate so we can move ahead on this opportunity.

It takes me half an hour to get into work. By the time I sit down at my desk, I already have responses to my post in my activity stream. One of the responses says, "I'm not available, but we just recently completed a similar document that we haven't posted to the Knowledge Exchange (the company's internal knowledge management database) yet, but here's a link to the document, you can grab it and reuse it."

Then someone else replies to the post and says, "I'm actually certified in that search product, and I'm looking for a project. How can I help?"

So literally within a half an hour, the problem is being solved. And by the way, the first person to respond is in Oslo and second guy is in New York. And I'm in Chicago!

Steven also uses Accenture's social site to find the information assets he needs to move forward with projects assigned directly to his team. Recently, for example, he and his colleagues were working on a company-wide portal upgrade project, and they needed to compare the features available in SharePoint 2010 (Microsoft's collaboration and social media platform) with the features in the previous version.

I wanted to know if anybody in the company had done any comparisons that summarized from our perspective the differences in capabilities between the older version and the newer version of SharePoint.

So I posted a brief description of what I was looking for and copied it to three communities on our social site— our portal community, our SharePoint community, and our Microsoft community.

By the end of the day, I got this great PowerPoint deck that someone in the company had already put together for a client who wanted to know the exact same thing— what's new about SharePoint 2010, which new features do we need, which features should we be using, etc. It had a fantastic breakdown showing me the exact points I was looking for.

Even more important, it saved me from duplicating all the work that someone else in the company had already done.

Steven predicts that future iterations of social media will include intelligent search features that will automatically create lists of experts throughout the enterprise who can pitch in and contribute when someone posts a request for support or assistance.

We're looking for full integration of our search engine into our social media platform and vice versa, so that when I post something, the search engine will bring me back results immediately, based on what I've asked.

So instead of doing a post and then a search, I can do both at the same time, and I will automatically see a list of people who are experts in the subject I'm researching, and I'll even see a list of their colleagues and the people they work with across the company. That will be very useful.

## ACCELERATING PRODUCT DEVELOPMENT

At salesforce.com, social media helps pick up the pace of product development processes, compressing activities that would normally unfold over weeks or months into hours or days.

Naturally enough, the company uses its own social collaboration technology, Salesforce Chatter, to solicit ideas and feedback from all areas of the business. Sean Whiteley, the company's vice president of product marketing, shared this story with us about his use of Chatter to accelerate the introduction of a design enhancement to the product itself:

> This morning, I'm designing some comps for one of our upcoming Chatter products. We have a product design team, we also have a marketing design team and we have various user experience teams. Lots of different people who come from many different camps. . . .
>
> I posted images of two comps on Chatter and asked, "What do you think of these comps? Give me the pros and cons."
>
> I got an unbelievable amount of feedback. Within an hour, I got feedback from about 40 people. A lot of the people who commented, I didn't even know. But within an hour, I had basically gotten feedback from across the entire company. And it all stacked up drastically in favor of one of the comps.
>
> For me, this was great. Now I didn't have to run around to all the different teams, compile all the results, compare them against one another. I just read through the comments on my post and I could see immediately what people wanted. Now I could move on to something else.
>
> We called this "crowd sourcing a design principal." It's much better than having a focus group. I don't like focus groups anyway. I need more than a focus group. I'd rather let the "mob" decide, especially when you have a product that's not ready for the public yet. What's also really useful about this approach is that you get a very wide variety of feedback. You don't just get feedback from someone who, for example, designs user flows all day long, and who might look at a new product very differently from the person who might actually use the product and who doesn't immediately understand what this new thing is supposed to do.

## DRIVING KNOWLEDGE INTO AND ACROSS THE ORGANIZATION

Institutional knowledge. Now, there's a term that makes you want to stop reading, rub your eyes, and take a long walk somewhere. We only use it to make a point and we promise not to use it again. Here's the point: The greatest challenge facing any organization is making sure that everyone knows what they have to know to get their jobs done properly.

There's a whole practice devoted to solving this challenge. It's called knowledge management. Traditionally, the knowledge management function has been given short shrift. For a variety of reasons, knowledge management has never gotten the respect it needs and deserves in the modern organization.

That being said, social media is poised to revolutionize and completely transform the practice of knowledge management. Consider this simple scenario: Your company makes headsets for wireless phones. You release a new version of the headset, but for some technical reason it doesn't pair with certain kinds of mobile phones. Your contact center is quickly overwhelmed with complaints from frustrated customers.

In the old days, this situation would have created a veritable cascade of challenges. First, depending on the quality of your contact center operations, it might take a while for you to become aware that you had a problem.

Then more time would pass between the moment when you became aware of the problem and the moment you develop a solution. Next, you would have to figure out a way for explaining the solution to your customer-facing agents and reps so that they, in turn, could explain the solution to your customers.

Wow, that's a lot of work—and there are plenty of cracks and crevices you can fall through before your customers are happy again.

Now let's reimagine that scenario in a socially networked universe. Some of your customers might actually contact your contact center, but a lot them will express their frustration via Twitter or some other form of microblogging. Someone at your company will quickly pick up the tweets or microblogs because they have set their social media feeds to search automatically for any mention of your company or its products.

Here's the really cool part: Before you've even had a chance to inform your product development team about the problem with the new headset, an individual, or several individuals, living out there in the social media universe will have seen the tweets from your customers, figured out a fix (or several fixes), tweeted the fixes, and—voila!—your problem is solved without you lifting a finger.

This, by the way, is an example of crowd sourcing, which relies on the combined problem-solving talents of large numbers of people. James Surowiecki describes this uncanny phenomenon in his excellent book, *The Wisdom of Crowds*.

Meanwhile, the cranky headset scenario continues unfolding. Assuming again that you have a social media strategy in place, the fixes suggested by the crowd are automatically pulled into your company's knowledge base, where they will be available to anyone in the company who needs them.

You can even automate a process for routing details about the fix directly to any customer-facing agents or reps who are likely to be dealing with complaints or questions from customers who bought headsets but who didn't see the fix on Twitter.

Now the crowd-sourced fix is part of your company's institutional memory, and it's available to the people who need it. That's the new face of knowledge management, baby!

## CROWD SOURCING . . .

Best Buy has become good at finding innovative, unorthodox methods for leveraging social media. One outstanding example is the company's "Twelpforce" service, which encourages Best Buy employees to interact directly with customers via Twitter. The employees answer product questions, troubleshoot technology challenges, and solve customer service issues, according to Barry Judge, Best Buy's chief marketing officer.

Here's an excerpt from a blog post announcing the initiative's launch in 2009. In the post, titled "Twelpforce—Blurring the lines between Customer Service and Marketing," Judge hints at the transformational/disruptive nature of the company's new initiative:

> I think that Twelpforce can be a catalyst to think very differently across our company about customer service. No longer do we need to passively wait in our channels for people to come to us. With Twelpforce specifically and social media in general we can actively seek out the conversations that increasingly are happening outside our channels. I also think this initiative can change our definition of customer service. No longer is customer service a department but something that all of us can do. And Twelpforce begins to really blur the lines between customer service and more traditional one-way marketing communications.

Best Buy is also an innovator in the use of internal social media to modernize parts of the traditional human resources function. For example, Best Buy customers are encouraged to post comments and share ideas on a site called Idea X. When the company posted the description for a new job, senior manager of emerging media marketing, customers posted their own ideas for how the job description should be written.

Judge wrote his own post about the ideas and cited what he considered to be the best contributions. Some of the ideas were incorporated into the subsequent versions of the official job description.

Not only is this a great illustration of how crowd-sourcing can be applied to an internal business process; it's a wonderful example of how practically any business process, no matter how intrinsically dull, can be turned into a successful marketing exercise with just a little bit of imagination.

The customers who posted comments were engaged and enthusiastic—it seemed as if they were *absolutely thrilled* to be helping Best Buy sort through a process that many people would find extremely and excruciatingly boring.

It's almost as if Best Buy were channeling Tom Sawyer's talent for convincing his friends and neighbors to help him whitewash Aunt Polly's fence.

And, of course, that is precisely the attribute of social media that gives it such power and potential: It's a great way for distributing large amounts of work (albeit mostly knowledge work) over a virtually inexhaustible pool of labor.

Outsourcing? Hah, you haven't seen anything yet! Social media will blow the doors off of outsourcing.

Visit one of HP's online Business Support Forums or Consumer Support Forums. Chances are good that your question will be answered by an unpaid volunteer or by several unpaid volunteers. HP has a history of encouraging its employees to work as unpaid volunteers in the Open Source community, but the concept is definitely contagious.

For example, Verizon Communications "employs" a small army of online technical experts to answer questions from customers ranging from how to reboot a wireless Internet router to the best ways for boosting the bass in a home theater's sound system.

"Employs" isn't really the right word because Verizon's online help forums are staffed by volunteers. Not just any volunteers, mind you, but so-called superusers who really dig the technology and want to share their knowledge with the world.

Verizon's volunteer-staffed site is managed by Lithium Technologies, which manages similar sites for AT&T, Linksys, Nintendo, and Best Buy.

The company's cofounder, Lyle Fong, told the *New York Times* that the superusers recruited for the help sites are highly respected— "revered" is actually the word he used in an interview with tech reporter Steve Lohr. These superusers are the leading edge of the new economy hinted at in Benkler's visionary book—an economy in which money and material wealth are less important than honor, respect, and the feeling of being useful.

Maybe that's the overarching takeaway—the networked economy is not just about money. Another way of saying this might be that there are multiple drivers in a networked economy, and money is just one of those drivers.

On some visceral level, executives tend to understand this—and it frightens some of them because it means they have to figure out a whole new set of motivational tools to keep employees productive.

Ironically, social media is emerging as one of those tools.

## WE'RE ALL HACKERS NOW

For most people, the word "hacker" summons up the image of a malevolent bearded basement-dwelling nerd armed with a roomful of expensive computer gear and bent on global destruction until his evil intentions are flummoxed by Bruce Willis or Steven Seagal.

For a new generation of *digerati*, however, the word conjures up an entirely different meaning. Hackers are inventors, explorers, pioneers, innovators. They are people who look at technology, take it apart, and try to make it better—or different, which in today's trend-driven markets is a prerequisite for better.

In a networked economy anchored in digital technologies, hacking is a critical vector for innovation. From the perspective of the telecoms, Skype was a hack. From Microsoft's perspective, the entire Open Source project is one giant ongoing hack.

Hacking is more than a sport or hobby, it's the new ethos. All of us operating in the social media universe are either hackers, hacker tourists (to steal a phrase from Neal Stephenson), or both.

The Internet is the platform (think of it, if you must, as hardware); the ideas we create and share are the software. Everything that we blog, tweet, or text is a hack.

In the old days, you needed a printing press if you wanted to share your ideas with the rest of the world. Now all you need is a keypad connected to the Internet.

# CHAPTER 3

# The Social Enterprise

*It's not a panacea; it's a strategy that takes into account how dramatically people have changed.*

—Paul Greenberg

## FORGET MURPHY'S LAW

The old corporation was all about command and control. Corporations were organized into hierarchies; orders and instructions flowed down from the top.

Management assumed that most employees were lazy and self-indulgent. As a consequence of this belief, management focused its energy on goading or coercing employees into working. Management assumed that all resources were scarce. As a consequence of this belief, management focused its energy on conserving or hoarding the company's resources.

Haunted by the idea of Murphy's Law, management assumed that anything and everything that *could* go wrong *would* go wrong.

As a result of these beliefs, the practice of management became a nonstop drill in risk avoidance. Disaster lurked behind every corner, change was always for the worse, and the only salvation lay in strict adherence to a carefully codified set of rules, processes, and procedures that were all designed to keep people from screwing up.

The new corporation is built on a very different premise. The whole notion of "command and control" is seen now as a relic of the past. Management (what's left of it, at any rate) generally accepts the idea that most people, when offered the opportunity, actually *want* to work. Most of the managers that we know understand that most of the people they manage actually *want* to be productive.

Talk to the managers at any large modern corporation and they'll tell you that the typical twenty-first-century worker wants to collaborate, wants to share, wants to feel needed, and wants to be part of a team. Most of all, the typical worker wants to feel appreciated and valued.

Despite the turmoil and upheaval of the past two or three decades, a steady evolution has been occurring in the relationship between employers and employees. The last vestiges of the feudal era (*I* am the king and *you* are my vassal, so do as I command thee . . . or else!) are falling by the wayside.

To the consternation and surprise of many doomsayers, the world economy has not crumbled. In fact, just the opposite has happened. Even with its gargantuan problems and staggering inequalities, the world economy is stronger than it has ever been, at any time in the past!

## MORE IMPORTANT THAN *MONEY*?

Back in the 1980s, when the idea of the "home office" came into vogue, the initial response of most managers was "No way! How will I know they're really working?"

Fast forward to the present. IBM employs more than 400,000 people in 170 countries. About 40 percent of IBM's workforce does not work in an IBM office. About 73 percent of the company's managers work remotely from the people they manage. Colocation is just no longer an issue at IBM.

Gone are the days when if you couldn't actually see someone toiling away at a desk, you had to assume that he or she wasn't working. That mode of thinking is just no longer valid. Why? What happened?

Here's part of the answer: In advanced economies such as ours, money by itself is no longer the dominating force that motivates people to work. Today, people work for a variety of reasons that have very little to do with money. They work to achieve status, recognition, independence, self-fulfillment, self-actualization, self-esteem—a whole bunch of abstract goals that would have struck our grandparents as wildly irresponsible and completely irrational reasons for working.

Back in the days when most people worked *only* for the money they earned, it was entirely reasonable for managers to expect the worst and to assume that most people would try to do the least amount of work in exchange for the most amount of money.

As the saying goes, if you always expect the worst, that's usually what you'll get. And that's precisely what management got: a well-paid, underperforming workforce.

For a multiplicity of reasons, that arrangement gradually became untenable. The idea of paying millions and millions of people to perform meaningless repetitive tasks in huge office buildings now strikes us as irresponsible and irrational.

Today we live in a radically different sort of economy. People are different, corporations are different, and the glue holding people and corporations together is different.

Now that so many people no longer work exclusively for money, a new attractive force has appeared. It's not loyalty, because most people don't work long enough in one place to develop deep feelings of loyalty. It's not some old-fashioned sense of personal ambition, because most workers understand reflexively that they are not in line to become the next Bill Gates or Meg Whitman.

The attractive force—the glue holding people and corporations together—is the sense of opportunity. People want to work for companies that they believe will offer them opportunities to feel good about what they are doing, feel good about the contributions they are making, and feel good in general about the quality of their lives.

If it sounds to you like we're saying that a growing number of people in today's economy are working so they can feel good about themselves—well, you heard us right. That's exactly what we're saying.

This increasingly large slice of the workforce looks for companies that understand the goals and aspirations of the Millennial Generation. Many of these workers aren't looking for a 9-to-5 job with a defined-benefits package—they're looking for opportunities to collaborate with other people on projects and assignments that are cool, different, challenging, and fun.

The fact that a lot of this type of work can be performed from any location with a high-speed Internet connection represents much more than just a temporary bonus for employers. It's an opportunity for employers all over the world to drastically reduce their overhead costs while substantially increasing the size of the available talent pool.

For example, until recently, if your company headquarters was in Manhattan, your cost of labor would be much higher than if your company was located in Abilene. In a socially networked economy, you can hire workers in Abilene—or anywhere, for that matter—at a fraction of the cost you would have paid for those same workers in New York.

## THE SOCIAL WORKFORCE

As you have probably noticed, the newer breed of employee spends a considerable amount of time on social media sites. If you've got a hankering for labels, you could call this new generation of employees the "social workforce"—because significant portions of their waking lives revolve around interactions taking place on social media platforms.

If you are restricting access to social sites during work hours, you are sending the wrong message to the social workforce. It's almost as if you're saying "We don't approve of your lifestyle." That kind of message seems unlikely to inspire optimal performances from your employees. And it is guaranteed to make some people think twice about going to work for you. After all, who would want to work at a place that restricts or forbids a basic kind of social interaction? Such a place would seem downright antisocial, right?

It's also important to remember that the lives of your customers also revolve around social media, so restricting employee access to social media will make it more difficult for you to find out what your customers are saying about you. Restricting employee access to social media is like poking yourself in the eye and shooting yourself in the foot—at the same time!

Here are two net takeaways that you need to consider:

1. If your company cannot connect to the social workforce on the right emotional wavelength, you will find it increasingly difficult to attract the kind of talent required to stay competitive in modern markets. In other words, nobody will want to work at your company.

2. If you aren't providing your workforce with a social networking platform, they won't be able to work as productively or as efficiently as workers at companies that are providing these kinds of resources for their workers.

## COLLABORATION IS THE NEW EFFICIENCY

Back in the 1980s, the adjective "smart" was widely applied to familiar products whose capabilities were enhanced or improved by adding miniaturized digital processors. There are smart cars, smart homes, smart bombs, and so on. Then in the 1990s, as more highly sophisticated software was developed and added to some of these products, "smart" was replaced by "intelligent."

The new adjective du jour is "social," and we're going to apply it now to describe organizations that have recognized (or are beginning to recognize) the value of social networking as a productivity engine. These pioneering organizations are inventing the next era of corporate evolution, the Era of the Social Enterprise.

But just calling something a social enterprise doesn't make it one. All corporations are aggregations of structures and frameworks created to enable the completion of tasks and processes that are considered essential to the business.

So instead of saying "Hey, our enterprise should be more social," let's start by looking at the components of the enterprise and figuring out which of them is a good fit for social initiatives that generate the best return on investment (ROI) with the fewest headaches. In other words, let's take a practical, commonsense approach to creating a social enterprise.

The social enterprise accepts the idea that people want to collaborate, want to work together, and want to solve problems. For the social enterprise, the big challenge isn't trying to figure out the best ways to entice or coerce their employees into working; the big challenge is providing employees with the social tools they need to collaborate.

The basic technology platform required to construct a social enterprise is, not surprisingly, social computing. The good news is that assembling the right set of social computing tools is a lot easier and a lot less expensive than maintaining a permanent layer of management whose primary focus is making sure that workers don't goof off or steal paperclips.

## SOCIAL HR

The process of finding a job often begins with the preparation of a resume listing your skills, qualifications, and experience. Then you send your resume to the human resources (HR) departments at dozens or perhaps hundreds of traditional companies, hoping that through some stroke of good fortune, your combination of skills, qualifications, and experience will match the needs of at least one of those companies.

The HR departments at the traditional companies receiving your resume are also hoping to find good matches. But they are also looking to avoid potential trouble, so they erect protective barriers that make it exceedingly difficult for them to gauge how well you actually will perform after they hire you.

As a result, the job-hunting and hiring process becomes a strange game in which both sides play blindfolded. That's not exactly a recipe for success.

The social enterprise sees collaboration as an asset and places a high value on the collaborative talents of its employees. Collaboration requires the ability to form trusting relationships, and forming trusting relationships requires social skills.

Naturally, the social enterprise wants to hire people with great social skills. The best way to find people with great social skills is by looking on social networking platforms.

The social enterprise also understands that its employees aren't just people sitting at desks, typing on keyboards, and staring into screens. The social enterprise sees its employees as representatives of the company brand.

"Companies today are brand-driven," says Laurie Ruettimann, an HR consultant and blogger.

> We live in a very brand-conscious world, and many of the conversations about your brand take place on social media sites. So it makes sense to hire brand-conscious, brand-savvy people who can interact with customers on every level, including social media. These days, it only takes a couple of tweets to kill your brand.

On the other side of the coin, an army of social employees can act as a multiplier force, spreading the word about new products and services much more efficiently than any marketing or PR campaign.

Says Laurie:

> With that in mind, HR departments can create talent management strategies to identify, hire, and retain individuals who will effectively evangelize your brand across the marketplace.

## FIRST IMPRESSIONS COUNT

Most prospective employees will start their job search by looking at the career pages of your corporate Website. For many people, your career pages will be the official "face" of your company—and as you know, you only get one chance to make a first impression.

If you're looking to hire brand-savvy people with social media skills, then your career pages need to project the look and feel of a company that cherishes its brand and understands social media.

Your career pages are also critical elements of your brand, and they will speak volumes to the employees that you want to hire. We recently asked Laurie to chat with us about the complicated relationship between brand cultivation and social media. Here's a snippet of her observations:

> Organizations that have aggressively worked to define their employment brand, such as The Container Store and Wegmans, a regional supermarket chain, know the value of a good career Website.

> Once an organization brands itself as a "Best Company to Work For," the benefits of social HR become evident. Consumers and job seekers flock to the corporate career website, creating a de facto social network.

> If moderated properly by a smart community manager, the career website becomes a rich database of information that can be mined for consumer sentiment. You can poll visitors and provide unique consumer offers from your career pages. There's great potential there that social HR can tap and turn into business advantages.

Social HR amplifies the power of traditional HR, turning it into a competitive asset, says Laurie.

> The sharpest organizations, such as Sodexo and EMC, employ recruiters and sourcers who gather both business *and* candidate intelligence in the marketplace. They have mastered social tools and they know their competitors—and who's working for their competitors—inside and out.

> In general, recruiters and sourcers are speaking to the best candidates out there. In the process, these HR professionals are learning important information about their respective industries that can be shared internally with marketing, sales, and PR for a competitive advantage.

Laurie represents a new generation of HR practitioners who play by the rules but know how to leverage the capabilities and reach of social technologies to dramatically improve the results of their efforts. She also believes strongly that when supported with the right social computing tools, HR can contribute meaningfully to the bottom line.

> Consumers are job seekers and job seekers are consumers. A conversation with consumers and job seekers no longer happens on commercials during the nightly newscasts. Conversations are happening on social websites.

> If you want to attract the best and the brightest employees in the marketplace, the corporate infrastructure that supports the HR strategy in your organization must evolve.

Companies that compete in rapidly changing markets need to hire people who can keep pace with those markets. "If your HR department is bogged down in a protracted discussion with your legal department about the risks of Facebook, you will miss an opportunity to hire and keep great employees who can move the market," says Laurie.

## THE TRAIN IS LEAVING THE STATION

While the idea of social HR might strike some as too "pie in the sky," it is already becoming a reality at many organizations. Smart companies that are evolving into social enterprises encourage social HR practices.

In other companies, however, social HR is emerging from the bottom up, as an unofficial grassroots effort without top-level support. That can lead to conflicts that likely will reduce productivity in the HR department and hamper the company's ability to attract and retain the best employees.

"In some situations, you have two HR departments," says Laurie.

> You have a traditional HR group acting as a compliance function, sort of a faux legal department. This group tends to be the most visible within the company because the people in it have positions of power and authority. Then you have a rogue HR group made up of people who are sick of the way traditional HR has operated for the past 30 years, and they are partnering with people in marketing, PR, and corporate communications and using their iPhones and their Facebook accounts to connect with talent.

By Laurie's estimation, comparing traditional HR to social HR is like comparing a biplane to a starship. "Social HR is a nexus of people-facing activities across the enterprise. We're just starting to realize the strategic potential of HR. This is only the beginning of the revolution."

Time will tell if Laurie is right. As you can probably guess, we're betting on her. If you are a senior executive at a company that depends on talent to stay competitive, we advise you to make some inquiries around your HR department and find out whether it's evolving in the right direction, or stuck in the past.

## THE NEW SOCIAL DIMENSION

Obviously, HR isn't the only functional area of the modern corporation that's transforming rapidly to keep pace with the socially connected world. Customer service, marketing, and public relations are also changing. What seems especially interesting, however, is how social networking has revealed a complex web of highly critical connections between these three areas. Without going into too much detail at this point, socially networked companies are noticing a shift in gravity from sales and marketing to customer service. In a very real sense, social networking has made a hash of the traditional relationships between the customer-facing areas of the modern corporation.

Gradually, a new set of relationships is emerging in which customer service exerts much greater influence over sales, marketing, and PR. Moreover, it seems that marketing is finally beginning to appreciate the incredibly rich potential of well-designed and well-executed customer relationship management (CRM) strategies.

Depending on your perspective, the combination of social networking and CRM either has brought the early visions of CRM thought leaders such as Don Peppers and Martha Rogers to fruition, or it has spawned a new and radically more powerful form of CRM.

Either way, this combination now makes it possible for CRM to reach new levels of effectiveness. It should come as no surprise that this new form of socially networked CRM has been dubbed "social CRM."

## SOCIAL CRM

Unlike "traditional" CRM, which mostly focused on getting information about customers into the hands of sales reps, social CRM focuses on gaining insight from the information created by customers (and communities of customers) when they interact with the companies they purchase goods and services from *and* when they interact with each other.

This is a critical point of differentiation between the *old* CRM and the *new* CRM. Although CRM's early proponents envisioned it as a philosophy and a strategy designed to improve human interactions in a business environment, the *old* CRM was mostly about using transactional information stored in a database to sell more stuff. The *new* CRM (i.e., social CRM) is more about figuring out what your customers really want and then anticipating their needs. This is a significant difference.

Brent Leary is a business technology consultant whom we respect. In a 2009 article in *Inc.*, Brent wrote that "social CRM is not a substitute, but a much-needed complement to traditional areas of customer relationship management. It gets us close to what we've needed all along."

Paul Greenberg is considered the preeminent philosopher of CRM. A well-traveled speaker and consultant, he is the author of *CRM at the Speed of Light* and writes a popular blog on the subject. We caught up with Paul recently and asked him to describe the difference between traditional CRM and social CRM. Here are snippets of his responses:

> Traditional CRM is very left-brained in a lot of ways. There are metrics and benchmarks and KPIs [key performance indicators] that you associate with it. Early CRM was mostly sales force automation. It was an "inside-out" approach to your customers. You built operational capability that enabled you to understand a bit more about your customers so you could optimize the product offerings for them. That, in a really brief nutshell, is traditional CRM.

> Social CRM starts from a somewhat different standpoint. It says that customer strategy has to move from the *operational* and *transactional* to the *interactional*.

The customer strategy is now one of engagement, because customer demands and behaviors have changed over the last six or seven years.

Social CRM takes customer input into account. It helps you understand what customers are thinking. Remember, the customers aren't necessarily thinking within the channels you own. They're working in different channels that you *don't* own. What they're saying about you and the conversations they're having about you—you don't own those either.

Now you have a situation where the customer runs the business ecosystem and your job as a company is to understand the change in customer behavior and understand that customers now control the business ecosystem.

So you have to provide the kind of interactions that the customers want. That doesn't mean just going out and building a Facebook page. It actually means optimizing your customer strategy and engaging your customers in ways that create *advocates*. The optimal goal is creating *advocates*, not satisfied customers.

From a sales and marketing perspective, this certainly amounts to a sea change in attitude. It implies an entirely new set of relationships between companies and their customers. It also reveals new cracks in the corporate edifice. In the old days, the customer was someone who stood outside the company, gazing in. In the social enterprise, the customer is invited inside to join the party.

Transformations such as those described by Paul and other CRM thought leaders tempt us to use the phrase "paradigm shift," but we'll spare you the agony. Suffice it to say that social CRM is the visible manifestation of a profound and probably permanent alteration in the way companies and customers relate. Here is how Paul describes the changing landscape:

We're really seeing two trends there. One is the integration of sales and marketing. The other is the growing dominance of customer service. As relationships evolve from *transactional* to *interactional*, customer service is becoming the wrapper around sales and marketing.

> Customers are saying to companies, "We need you to tell
> us more about your company so that we can make
> intelligent decisions about how we want to deal with
> you."

> That's a huge shift from the past, when companies said to
> customers, "Here is the product or service—live with it."
> Now the customer is saying, "No, I'm not going to live
> with it. In fact, I want you to expose much more
> information so that I can determine for myself what I
> want to do with you as a company."

Paul and others see social CRM as the framework for new and improved relationships between buyers and sellers—relationships in which buyers dominate a vast ecosystem of interconnected markets and economies. Says Paul:

> It's not a panacea; it's a strategy that takes into account
> how dramatically people have changed. In the past,
> customers were outsiders in the business ecosystem. Now
> they're insiders in the business ecosystem. That's a big
> difference.

## SOCIAL LEADERSHIP

If Paul Greenberg is the Bob Dylan of CRM, then Charlene Li is the Lady Gaga of social media. Charlene is the founder of the Altimeter Group, a fast-rising consulting firm that specializes in interactive marketing. Previously she was a vice president and principal analyst at Forrester Research and a consultant at Monitor Group. She was named one of the 12 Most Creative Minds of 2008 by *Fast Company* and one of the Most Influential Women in Technology in 2009. In 2010, she was named one of *Fast Company*'s 100 Most Creative People in Business.

We're recapping the details of Charlene's career so you understand that in the social media universe, she truly *is* a rock star. If you haven't read her books, we urge you to do so immediately. Her new book, *Open Leadership*, is aimed at managers and executives who are struggling to find their way in the new socially networked economy. Although *Open Leadership* focuses more on the positive aspects of this brave new world, careful readers will note the book's many subtle warnings.

In a section titled "The Leader's Dilemma," Charlene observes that enlightened modern executives are asking themselves the same question that vexed enlightened medieval kings: How do you loosen the reins of control without losing control?

This isn't an idle or speculative question—finding the correct answer is the key to success in today's ultra-competitive, supertrendy, and continually shifting markets. As Charlene notes, "You can't simply 'Six Sigma' your way into new markets."

The traditional approach to leadership is under crushing pressure to change for two reasons, she writes.

> First, the parameters of success have changed from
> process control to innovation. . . . Second, businesses are
> now more likely to be delivering services than
> manufacturing objects. A skilled and motivated workforce
> on the front lines quickly chafes under strict limitations
> and hierarchies, unable to do what they think is needed
> because of headquarters' disconnected notions of what
> really works in the market.

While in the past leaders relied on clearly articulated and rigidly disciplined organizational structures to make sure that their commands were carried out, today's markets evolve far too quickly for those kinds of iron-clad and heavily bureaucratized leadership frameworks.

> . . . good management meant strict adherence to
> predetermined measures of success. In addition, the high
> cost of communications and information meant that only
> the most precious, important information moved up and
> down corporate hierarchies—leaders relied on a clear
> "chain of command," and any information that flowed
> outside of that chain was slapped down.

Charlene offers five "new rules of open leadership" for modern corporate leaders:

1. Respect that your customers and employees have power.
2. Share constantly and build trust.

3. Nurture curiosity and humility.

4. Hold openness accountable.

5. Forgive failure.

Again, we urge you to read Charlene's books. Then you can really appreciate her arguments and draw your own conclusions. If you're thinking about social media strategy, Charlene is a great resource.

## MAKING IT STICK

In 2008, IBM released the third edition of its biennial Global CEO Study series. The information in the study, according to IBM, was based on "in-person interviews with 1,130 CEOs, general managers and senior public sector and business leaders from around the world."

The study was titled "The Enterprise of the Future," and it lived up to its name. Here are the top three bullets from the executive summary page of the study:

- **Organizations are bombarded by change, and many are struggling to keep up.** Eight out of ten CEOs see significant change ahead, and yet the gap between expected change and the ability to manage it has almost tripled since our last Global CEO Study in 2006.

- **CEOs view more demanding customers not as a threat, but as an opportunity to differentiate.** CEOs are spending more to attract and retain increasingly prosperous, informed and socially aware customers.

- **Nearly all CEOs are adapting their business models—two-thirds are implementing extensive innovations.** More than 40 percent are changing their enterprise models to be more collaborative.

A close reading of the study does indeed reveal a widespread sense that the pace of change in various markets, all over the world, has accelerated to such a degree that traditional businesses, weighed down by their traditional processes, are simply not up to the job of responding.

As part of its own business transformation, IBM launched an internal campaign to increase the adoption of social computing within the company. The campaign, known as "BlueIQ," is led by a small core of managers. In addition to its core team, BlueIQ has enlisted another 1,400 or so volunteer "ambassadors" to spread the word about social computing inside and outside the company.

"We call it 'BlueIQ' because we're trying to raise the collective intelligence of IBM," says Jeanne Murray, who serves as one of BlueIQ's leaders.

Jeanne and her colleague, Rawn Shah, are the coauthors of a useful white paper, "Nurturing BlueIQ: Enterprise 2.0 Adoption in IBM." In the white paper, Jeanne and Rawn examine the "glories and frustrations" of IBM's efforts to increase the levels of practical collaboration across its enormous organization through the increased use of social tools.

Boiled down to its essentials, the white paper offers a handy guide of dos and don'ts for large organizations contemplating social computing initiatives.

For example, Jeanne and Rawn note that adoption depends on more than installing a new set of software tools. "While technology is a core component, adoption requires a focus on people, behaviors and processes," they write.

In their white paper, Jeanne and Rawn offer a concise list of success factors that includes:

- Focus on open collaboration across the complete organization, and not just . . . to individuals, groups, or organizational units.

- Get leadership buy-in at the highest levels, but also at the middle-management level.

- Recruit an enthusiastic, representative population of evangelists; arm them with educational material; and legitimize their individual contributions as part of the overall adoption effort.

- Continually communicate your program goals, tactics, and activities to gain mindshare across the organization.

*Source: Nurturing BlueIQ: Enterprise 2.0 Adoption in IBM*

They also note that because "adoption depends on the behaviors and interactions of people, you will need to provide guidelines and governance as part of your adoption program."

This is certainly reasonable advice, and it corresponds to our own experiences in promoting social media programs. The second half of this book is devoted mostly to listing, explaining, and discussing the various tactics and processes necessary for developing and managing a successful social media strategy. In this first half of the book, which dwells more on the overall phenomenon of enterprise social media, we're painting the issues and challenges in broader strokes.

Three of these broad-stroke issues concern the choice of tools, varying levels of comfort with the whole idea of social media, and the role of evangelists in the early stages of rolling out corporate social media initiatives. We decided to touch on these issues now because Jeanne brought them to our attention in a telephone conversation that we had with her not long after we read the white paper.

The challenge with tools, she told us, is that many people have already developed their own notions of what social media tools should look and feel like. But these notions depend on the individual, and so they can vary widely. One person might think that a corporate social media interface should resemble Facebook, while someone else might think it should resemble Google Docs. Others might think it should be like Flickr, Wikipedia, MySpace, LinkedIn, Twitter, or YouTube.

It would be a gross mistake to believe that because many people are already familiar with similar tools, the deployment of a corporate social media tool will be a trouble-free experience. If the rollout of the tool itself is problematic, adoption of the social media initiative is likely to be problematic also. Here is Jeanne's no-nonsense take on the matter of tools:

> From the perspective of an IT manager or an infrastructure manager, implementation of a new tool is a pretty straightforward deal. You pilot the tool, then you roll it out, and then you make everybody use it.
>
> But in the social area, people don't necessarily adopt a new tool just because it's there. If they don't like it, they won't use it or they'll find something else they like.

That has been one big difference that we discovered with
these social collaboration tools. You can't just mandate
that people use them. In addition to having good tools in
the first place, you also have to make sure that people
understand why they are being asked to use the tools
and what the tools can help them accomplish.

Today, everybody can go out to the Internet and use
social collaboration tools like Facebook and Twitter.
People will bring their experiences and their expectations
to the workplace, and that can complicate the
deployment of social tools.

Comfort levels with social collaboration tools can also vary widely.
In the same way that many people were wary of PCs when they were
initially introduced into the workplace, many people harbor suspi-
cions about social collaboration tools. Here is Jeanne again:

Behavior and culture will pose obstacles to change. You
will find inhibitors that slow the pace of adoption. Some
of these inhibitors are at the individual level and some
are at the organizational level. Some involve perceptions
that have no basis in reality, but whether their concerns
are real or not doesn't matter, you still have to address
them.

We found that the best way to address these challenges—
both in the area of tools and in the area of behavior and
culture—is to really focus on the business value. That
comes down to focusing on tasks that people are doing
and how they're getting their work done.

People might have all kinds of opinions, but the common
ground is that everybody's trying to get some business
done. That's the common ground where you have to
start—getting business done. Everybody can relate to
that. So that's where you start the conversations with
people and that's how you begin overcoming the
inhibitions and getting past some of the challenges.

At each stage of the initiative, new challenges and opportunities
surfaced. On the upside, marketing picked up on the value of social
collaboration very quickly. Many of the social tools eventually were
accepted more broadly, and evidence began to accumulate that the

tools were enabling faster work flows in various parts of the company. The general mind-set of the company gradually began shifting in favor of social collaboration, resulting in more "serendipitous" moments, faster execution by socially connected teams, improved knowledge flow, and higher levels of trust in peer capabilities.

On the downside, early adopters tended to be ignored or marginalized, some work flows changed unpredictably, participation was uneven across the company, and rivalries emerged between proponents of different tools. In more than one instance, the initiative seemed to underscore the old observation that new business processes don't translate easily into new thought processes. These challenges helped illuminate areas where the BlueIQ team needed to adjust the adoption program to match the everyday realities of the business, Jeanne notes.

Says Jeanne:

> It's important to remember that people aren't all coming from the same place and they will have different "sweet spots" of value when approaching social collaboration. Some people will find great value in the personal connections that they can make through social tools. Other people will be more interested in file-sharing capabilities. Some people will be happy if it helps them find a presentation that has been blessed by the product managers.

Jeanne warns against relying too much on early adopters and enthusiasts of new technology to "sell" social collaboration programs across the enterprise:

> I think one of the dangers here is that people who have already bought into the idea of social computing don't necessarily see it through the same eyes as the people who have not bought into it. So while the early adopters can be really helpful, they're not always sensitive to the inhibitions that others have. My advice is not to assume that everybody in the company places the same value on social computing collaboration.

The moral of the story, she says, is to focus on specific business tasks that can be made easier with social collaboration tools.

Starting with the tasks will help you narrow your scope. Then you can prioritize by finding the pain points. Wherever you're having the most pain, that's where you're likely to make the most progress. People need some kind of motivation to change their behavior and relieving pain is a good form of motivation. If you can show someone how social collaboration will make the pain go away, they will find a way to change their behavior and adapt to this new way of working.

## LEGAL NICETIES

Before leaving Part I of this book, we thought it wise to touch briefly on a topic that seems to bedevil some executives when they confront proposals for launching social media initiatives.

Like good managers, they start off by asking "What are the benefits? How will you measure success? How much will it cost? How many people will be involved? What's the ROI?"

But then they get caught up by their fear that somehow, someway, social media will open a Pandora's Box of legal issues. Some of this fear is normal and understandable. Some of it is just plain paranoia masquerading as corporate responsibility.

The shortest route out of this potentially time-wasting labyrinth is through your corporate legal department. By now, your chief counsel probably will have assigned someone to review any of the applicable laws or regulations, and he or she will be able to answer your questions and make suggestions for addressing any potential issues or problems. That's what corporate attorneys do for a living, and most of them are pretty good at it.

Teka Thomas, a Washington, D.C.–based attorney, says discussions about the legal consequences of social media usually revolve around topics such as

- Consumer protection
- Employment law
- Corporate security
- Litigation discovery
- Securities law

- Intellectual property
- Privacy
- Defamation

"This is all so new and so hot," says Teka.

> It touches many parts of the law. My general advice is to
> listen to your lawyers. Apply the same rules to social
> media that you apply to advertising and public relations.
> Don't deceive people, and be ready to back up whatever
> you say with facts.

Explain to your employees the difference between private and public information. Don't assume that every employee will be able to draw a clear line of demarcation between "business social media" and "personal social media." Create a short list of red-flag issues that might warrant a call to the corporate counsel.

And remember that the more you tweet, the more likely you are to be perceived as a public figure. For managers and executives who take their privacy for granted, becoming a public figure can be a distinctly unpleasant experience.

## HIGH SPEEDS NEED SEAT BELTS

We asked Christopher Gatewood, an attorney in Richmond, Virginia, who specializes in social media issues, to weigh in with his opinions about the best ways to allay management's fears of legal "consequences" resulting from corporate social media initiatives.

"First, I remind them that their customers and their potential customers are already there and waiting for them," says Chris. That usually puts the conversation on a firm business footing and reduces the level of anxiety.

> Then we talk about their fears and doubts. Some people
> are worried about defamation. Others are worried about
> releasing confidential or inaccurate information to the
> public. Some are worried that the tone of a blog might
> leave a bad taste in someone's mouth. You name it,
> people will worry about it. But that's how you start, by
> talking through everyone's fears and concerns. A little bit

of conversation and some risk management on the front
end is a good investment, because you can't put the
horse back in the barn later.

After the management team has discussed the risks and the benefits, it's easier to move forward with a social media strategy. The next
step is figuring out which people in the organization will be "depu-
tized" to participate in the social media initiative and putting together
a simple list of guidelines.

"You can't just give everyone a list of things they can't do. That's
not an effective strategy. It will drive everyone crazy," says Chris.
"They'll be so afraid of stepping in the wrong place that they won't
step anywhere."

Focusing exclusively on potentially negative outcomes is largely a
waste of time and resources, since "we all know there's a thousand
ways to mess something up," Chris observes.

Instead, he suggests:

> You want to figure out what you *can* do and what you
> *should* do with social media. You want to explain to
> people, "OK, here's what we *expect* you to do in this
> space." I hate using a sports analogy, but it's like a
> football field: There are lines around the field that show
> you clearly where the game is supposed to be played.
> If you can draw the lines for people and show them the
> boundaries, you're on your way to using social media
> productively.

While it would be foolish to completely ignore the potential
hazards of social media, it would be equally foolish to do nothing.

> One of the first things I say is "High speeds need seat
> belts." If you have clear policies, it will be easier for your
> employees to understand what's OK and what's not OK.
> You need to draw the lines so people can see where they
> can go, and where they can't go.

Don't underestimate the need for training and don't assume that
everyone in the organization will smoothly or automatically make the
leap from "personal" social media to "corporate" social media.

## TAKE THE TIME TO WRITE IT DOWN

We were fortunate to be introduced to Liza Emin Levitt, assistant general counsel at Intuit. Liza agreed that for social media initiatives, an ounce of prevention is definitely worth a pound of cure. She was also kind enough to share Intuit's social communications policy with us, and with her permission, we have included it in the Appendix. In addition to being an excellent template, it demonstrates how a great company articulates an important policy in positive, down-to-earth language that is clear and concise, without being harsh or threatening.

We will return to the topic of corporate social media policy in Part II of this book.

Part
**II**

---

# Building a Structure for Success

Big companies have a reputation for loving structure, committees, task forces, and reports. There's a reason for that. If you want to run a successful enterprise of more than one person, you need to know who is doing what when, and why they're doing it.

Social media, as a whole, began with individuals. If you think back to the dawning of the twenty-first century and imagine the early proto-bloggers, you're probably not picturing a corporate communicator but rather somebody in a darkened room, in a pizza-stained T-shirt bathed in the glow of a monitor, wondering if anybody is reading what he's posting. (At least one of your authors resembles that remark.)

Many of the people advocating for social media inside companies today were originally attracted to it for personal rather than professional reasons and only later recognized its value for business. The challenge for the enterprise is to emulate that spirit of adventure, community, and openness while at the same time keeping an eye on core business objectives and the bottom line.

The best way to do that is to build a structure inside your organization where social media can live, policies and guidelines for how employees can and should use it, and tools to measure its impact.

CHAPTER **4**

# Get Everybody Together in the Same Room

*If one does not know to which port one is sailing, no wind is favorable.*

—Lucius Annaeus Seneca

The first piece of advice we'll offer to anyone wanting to get social media off the ground in their company is "Get everybody together in the same room." Most companies have the early adopters who will frantically tell you that you're a year behind, the curmudgeons who still think social media is just a fad, and a lot of people in the middle who are interested and aware but don't know how it all works and fits in.

Plus, every company has stakeholders who want a say in how you'll move forward: marketing, public relations, the Web team, the IT department, HR, legal, and, if you're lucky, product development, customer service, and tech support.

You need to get them all involved for four reasons:

1. Any one of those groups has the potential to scuttle your social media adoption efforts before you get them off the ground.

2. Unless you work for a company with one employee, you can't possibly know all the ramifications yourself.

3. It's important to invite the skeptics as well as the evangelists. You'll find that the early adopters can help evangelize the cynics, and the cynics can bring a voice of reason for the people who want to dive in without thinking.

4. Finally, it's the right thing to do. Social media isn't a strategy in itself. It's a set of tools and a philosophy of how to communicate in a real and genuine manner in the ways that your audiences want to communicate. It touches every aspect of a company's business, and for it to succeed, it needs to be integrated across the enterprise.

## INVITE THE PRACTITIONERS, NOT JUST THE RULEMAKERS

Imagine something you're really passionate about doing in your spare time. One of the authors (Dave) really enjoys cooking, for instance, and likes buying new knives and pans and kitchen utensils. He has about a half dozen spatulas and isn't afraid to admit it. A few of those spatulas were obviously designed by people who have never so much as scrambled an egg. They look cool, but they don't actually work. The one Dave uses was clearly designed by a chef. In fact, it frequently shows up on the TV cooking shows. It's so well designed that it's like an extension of the hand.

There may well be people in your company who are just as excited about social media. They use it at home in their spare time. They can tell you the strengths and weaknesses of the various blog platforms and Twitter tools. They have up-to-date and complete profiles on LinkedIn, and they regularly shoot, edit, and post videos to YouTube.

You need to make sure those people are involved in setting your policies and guidelines. They can help you understand how social media tools are used in the real world. They can help you write your guidelines in a way that will make sense to the eventual users.

If you let your policies and guidelines be driven solely by the rule makers, they won't reflect the real world and they won't work. At best you'll find yourself rewriting them in a few months. At worst people will just ignore them.

## FIGURE OUT WHAT'S IMPORTANT

SAS got started by creating a group called the Marketing 2.0 Council that drew from the expertise of people from marketing to R&D and nearly everyone in between. It had strong executive leadership that helped get the council started. The council's first meeting was literally standing room only. Nearly 50 people came together to hear what the Marketing 2.0 Council was all about.

The very first thing the Marketing 2.0 Council did (after finding everybody a chair) was to decide what areas to address. Ask a group of ten people to define Web 2.0, Marketing 2.0, digital media, and social media, and you'll get something between ten different answers and a fistfight.

One early meeting, led by a professional facilitator, was designed solely to make a list of the specific areas under all those broad categories that were worth addressing. The team threw out suggestions and made a list on a flip chart of everything that came to mind, from blogs, to content syndication, to Second Life.

The next step was to narrow the focus. The group went through the list and voted for the ones they most wanted to keep. Those with no votes were crossed out. For items on the list that had only a few votes, people were given the opportunity to advocate for them. Once the process was complete, the group had consensus, and a list of six general topic areas:

1. Blogs
2. Social networks
3. Content syndication
4. Video
5. Podcasts
6. Wikipedia

You'll notice Second Life did not make the cut. You'll also notice that Twitter isn't on that list. SAS created this list in 2007, when Twitter was still a glint in the geekiest of tech geeks' eyes. Since then it has been added

The Marketing 2.0 Council also came to another realization early on in the process: It doesn't matter how you share your content if you don't have good content to share, so Content was added to the list as an overarching category of its own.

The list has refined itself somewhat over the nearly three years since it was created. No topic area has been removed, but the way people at SAS use the different tools has realigned the priorities somewhat. When people at SAS look at social media tools, they are primarily concerned with blogs, social networks (LinkedIn and Facebook), Twitter, and YouTube.

A year from now, that list will no doubt be different. Location-based services like Foursquare, Gowalla, and TriOut are becoming more and more popular. As they did with Twitter at the outset, the social media early adopters are playing with them and learning how they work. The corporate marketers are never too far behind.

## WHAT ARE YOUR EXISTING GOALS?

Social media may be its own discipline right now, but in a corporate context, it really is just another facet of marketing communications, and it needs to be treated that way.

In order for your social media activities to have any chance of succeeding, you first need to make sure you have clear goals established for your communications activities. Are you trying to raise awareness of your company? Improve your brand reputation? Answer customer questions more quickly and efficiently? Fill your sales funnel with qualified leads? All of the above?

Again, social media is not a strategy in itself. It's a set of tools and a philosophy of communication. It's also not a quick fix; don't abandon things that are working in favor of social media tactics. As social media blogger and head of the Twist Image agency Mitch Joel says, "Everything is 'with,' not 'instead of.'"

Make sure you have a clear set of goals for your communications activities. Stick them up on the wall. Review them. Make sure they still make sense. Hang on to that list, because we'll talk more about mapping social media to your goals in a later chapter.

## WHAT MAKES SENSE IN YOUR INDUSTRY?

The way you approach your social media guidelines—and your social media strategy in general—will depend in a large part on what kind of industry you're in. Social media can be equally beneficial for big companies, small companies, business to consumer (B2C) companies, and business to business (B2B) companies, but your particular industry will govern your approach to a certain degree.

If you're a consumer packaged goods company looking to introduce a new product to 18- to 24-year-old consumers of high fructose corn syrup pressed into interesting shapes, your market will dictate one approach. If you're a B2B technology company hoping to influence the decision-making process of CIOs, you'll have a different approach.

Likewise, if you're in a highly regulated industry like pharma, you're going to have your own set of challenges. Make sure your approach to social media makes sense in your industry. If you're lucky, other companies in your industry have blazed a trail, and you can learn from what they've done. If you're really lucky, your industry trade group may be able to provide you some guidance.

## WHAT MAKES SENSE IN YOUR COMPANY?

In addition to understanding what makes sense in your industry, you need to give some thought to what makes sense in your own company. What has your communications style been up to this point? Are you casual and open, or are you close-mouthed and cautious?

For your social media guidelines to make sense and be helpful, they need to take those realities into consideration. Zappos, for instance, encourages all employees to communicate with customers and help solve their problems, so the company has a very open approach to social media.

If that's not the way your company likes to communicate, don't try to force transparency and openness right off the bat. Make sure your policies are in line with the way your company and your employees feel comfortable communicating. But also get used to the idea that participating in social media is going to drive more openness.

## HOW CAN YOU FIGURE OUT WHAT WILL WORK FOR YOU?

If there's one thing corporate folks love, it's a committee. Even better, let's call it a task force so that we sound like we're maybe working with Jack Bauer on *24*.

SAS took its list of focus areas and created task forces for each one, headed by members of the Marketing 2.0 Council with responsibility or affinity for each area. The head of SAS's Video Communications and New Media team, for instance, led the YouTube task force.

The mission of each task force was to look at what SAS was already doing in each focus area, what the competitors were doing, find the best examples of companies using those channels, and present a set of recommendations for what the company should do.

That process took about eight weeks. The task force leaders presented their findings to the Marketing 2.0 Council, who asked questions—and started a few arguments—but the end result was a comprehensive set of directions agreed on by all parties.

As a result, every member of the council now had a much deeper understanding of the most important social media trends and channels and was equipped with the knowledge to spread the message inside the company.

## WHAT YOU CAN DO RIGHT NOW

- Identify the people in your company who are already active in social media.
- Create a Social Media Council.
- Make a list of what you're already doing in social media.
- Make a list of what your competitors are doing.
- Make a list of what the most innovative companies in your industry are doing.
- Look at your existing goals and see which ones could benefit from a social media component.

# CHAPTER 5

# Creating Social Media Guidelines

*Common sense is not so common.*

—Voltaire

One of the first major challenges SAS faced when creating social media policies was to take the task force reports and turn them into a set of guidelines and recommendations. More than just a set of employee social media policies, these guidelines needed to encompass not only the *what* of what SAS employees should be doing but also the *who* and the *how*.

The task force recommendations formed a solid base, and it was a relatively straightforward task to turn them into guidelines. Once you've identified what your goals are for social media and your company's readiness to participate and have looked at the areas you want to address, the hard work is done.

Even so, you need to make sure your guidelines address your employees' social media needs, and are presented in a way your employees will find practical and memorable.

Some companies have "crowdsourced" their social media policies, allowing employees to create and edit them on an internal Wiki. That is a bold and beautiful idea that fits perfectly into the ethos of social media. If you think that will work for your company, you'll identify a lot of potential objections and areas of confusion from the start.

## BE CLEAR AND CONCISE

As with any corporate document, it can be easy for your social media policies to stretch to page after page. Some corporate policies are long and cover lots of topics. Some companies feel comfortable limiting their policies to the admonition "Don't do anything stupid." (That approach may work in small companies but probably won't in a larger enterprise.)

Resist the urge to turn your social media policies into a comprehensive document that covers every eventuality. Keep in mind that you are asking busy people to read and digest new information. The more effectively you distill your key points into a form that is easy to read and remember, the more effective your policies will be.

One way to keep your policies concise is to consider what topics are already covered in your existing policies. Do you already have a computer use policy that prohibits your employees from visiting certain types of Web sites? If so, you can refer to those policies in your social media policy and not have to cover that ground again.

Do you already have HR policies that govern the way employees talk about the company or talk about their coworkers? Then you don't need to revisit those topics in your social media policy. Try to keep your social media policy focused, lively, informative, and concise.

In a perfect world, all of your employees read everything you send to them, file the message away for future reference, and follow all your policies to the letter.

In the real world, it pays to have something quick and easy to get the message across to busy people. You could even mark it "If you only read one social media policy message this year, read this one." But you probably won't.

## GUIDING PRINCIPLES FOR SOCIAL MEDIA AT SAS

One of the first things SAS employees saw when they opened the Social Media Guidelines and Recommendations was a set of guiding principles. The purpose of these principles was to give employees a high-level, mission statement–style overview of what to expect. Here they are:

> People are talking about SAS online whether we are there or not. It's good for SAS employees to participate in those conversations provided we do it in a way that is respectful of the standards of the online community, follows the Social Media Guidelines & Recommendations, the Online Conduct Guidelines, and behavior and computer use policies.

> We trust SAS employees to represent SAS online in a professional manner, the same way we trust them to do it in the real world.

> Don't talk about customers, partners or vendors, reveal private or proprietary information, intellectual property, pricing, details of customer installations or anything else that could harm our business or business relationships. The exception: You can link to content on sas.com that references customers, like success stories, press releases and videos.

> When you participate in social media, you are speaking for yourself, not on behalf of the company. Be sure to make that clear. And know that you are responsible for your actions.

> Talk to your manager about your social media activities, what you're doing, how it relates to your job and how much time you spend doing it.

> Open communication among employees, customers and the community at large will inevitably lead to some uncomfortable moments, but we can deal with those, and the benefits far outweigh the risk.

## INCLUDE DOS AS WELL AS DON'TS

Many of the people who will want a say in your corporate social media policies, from legal, to HR, to brand management, are worried about the potential negative impact social media can have. It's important to consider and address their concerns. But it's also important to make sure your policies don't scare people away. If you start off by outlining all the different ways social media can get an employee into trouble, you may be sabotaging your social media program before it gets off the ground.

If you want people to get excited about the potential of social media, be sure to include the dos as well as the don'ts. If you say, for instance, "Don't reveal proprietary company information in social media," be sure also to tell people they can use social media to highlight customer success stories and positive company news.

Many corporate social media policies advise employees to avoid polarizing subjects like politics and religion. That's a reasonable stipulation to make for employees using social media to communicate about their companies. But also be sure to let people know that it's OK to be themselves and let their personality show through, as long as they keep their activities inclusive rather than exclusive.

Make sure you strike a balance between the cautionary and encouraging so that the final result leaves people with a positive feeling about participating in social media.

Socialmediagovernance.com has created an online database of publicly available corporate social media policies, at http://socialmediagovernance.com/policies.php. If your company is just beginning to create policies, reading other companies' policies is a great way to start.

But don't just cut and paste. For your social media policies to truly work for your company, they need to reflect your goals and your corporate culture.

## INCLUDE EXAMPLES

"Show, don't tell" is a piece of advice often given to writers. People need a context to understand new and difficult concepts, and social media is no different. Instead of trying to tell people what makes a good tweet, for instance, show them examples of interesting and relevant tweets. Instead of telling them not to reveal proprietary information, show some examples of messages that share relevant and interesting information without revealing too much.

## COMMUNICATE AS OFTEN AS POSSIBLE, IN EVERY CHANNEL YOU HAVE

SAS released its Social Media Guidelines and Recommendations in June 2007. The guidelines covered everything from how to choose a user name to how to comment on a blog post with which you disagree. The guidelines clearly laid out what SAS employees could and could not do, and gave specific examples of how to use the major social media channels effectively as part of a communications and marketing campaign. They were written to encourage employees to feel comfortable participating in social media and let them know the company thinks it's a good thing.

SAS launched the guidelines with a front-page article on the SAS Wide Web global Intranet and an email blast to all managers. As social media manager, Dave spent the next six months going to team meetings large and small, in person and virtually, in the United States and Europe and Latin America and Asia. He spoke to marketers and PR folks and salespeople and Web managers and representatives from HR and training departments. He answered hundreds of emails from people with questions large and small.

Almost one year later, following that extensive and exhaustive communications campaign, a colleague stuck her head in Dave's door and said, "Quick question: Are we allowed to check Facebook while we're at work?"

No matter how good your social media policies are, they don't do you any good if no one knows they exist. Again, for those of you who work for companies with more than one employee, you know how hard it is to communicate something to everyone in your organization. Getting a consistent message to thousands of employees in dozens of countries is a major challenge.

The solution to that problem is to communicate as often as possible, in every channel you have. To communicate about social media, SAS uses an internal blog and publishes SAS Wide Web articles designed to highlight social media activities, advice, and best practices. There's also a training program designed to take employees from the most basic 101-level understanding of social media to more advanced topics, such as participating in LinkedIn groups and creating Twitter campaigns.

No matter how much you think you've communicated your social media policies and best practices, there's still someone out there who doesn't know what he or she can and can't do. Reaching that person is a constant challenge and one that can be met only by using all of the tools at your disposal and making social media a core element of your communications objectives.

You can read more about how some smart companies are sharing the social media message in Chapter 14 on the topic of internal communications.

## SPOTLIGHT SUCCESSES

One of the most effective ways to show employees the value of social media is to shine a spotlight on the successes of other people inside your company. Trying to get the attention of a busy salesperson can be a challenge, but show her how a colleague used Twitter to get a meeting with a key contact and suddenly you're speaking a language she can understand.

In Chapter 12, you'll meet Annette Green and Patty Hager from SAS. Annette and Patty are smart folks. When they saw that potential SAS customers were sharing information on LinkedIn and Twitter about the conferences they were attending, the business challenges they were facing, and the people they knew, Annette and Patty immediately saw the potential.

Dave went to Annette's office with a small video camera, shot a quick ten-minute interview with Annette and Patty about the ways they were using LinkedIn and Twitter to get useful information that helped them build connections and close deals, and posted it to the internal Marketing 2.0 Council blog.

Since then, quite a few people at SAS—salespeople and others—have seen that video, which showed them not only that it was OK to use social media at work but that it could also have real and immediate business value.

A quickly shot and roughly edited video interview with a general manager talking about the value of LinkedIn and Twitter was a far more effective tool in communicating social media's value to salespeople than any blog post or email blast, because the audience knew

Annette and Patty, shared the same goals and objectives, and spoke their language.

Find the people in your company who are doing social media right and let them tell the story to their colleagues in their own words.

## LEAD BY EXAMPLE

Ultimately, no matter how busy you are, the most effective way to understand social media and its impact on your business is to participate yourself. And it's also the most effective way to guide and motivate the people around you in your organization.

If you're a leader in your company and participating in social media, people in your organization will be watching you. Set a good example. That doesn't mean you have to be the first person to use every new technology, and it doesn't mean you have to set the world record for tweets per day. But it does mean you should be active and exemplify the standards you'd like your organization to follow. Whatever you and other leaders and trailblazers do in social media will be seen as setting the standard for your company.

All in all, it's a positive challenge. Dave has often said that he made a decision in 1994 when he first started communicating on the Internet that he would never say anything online that he wouldn't say face-to-face, and he's never regretted it.

Here's another goal you should set for yourself that might be hard to live up to (especially if you fly a lot): Never say anything negative online about other companies or brands. Anyone could be a customer, or a potential customer, and the last thing you want to do is use a positive and inclusive medium to alienate.

Again, we're finding that the core principles of social media aren't that different from the core principles of polite society. If you complain a lot in social media, you will quickly develop a reputation as a negative person. Do you think your employees, bosses, coworkers, customers, and potential customers enjoy working with negative people?

Not everyone follows this rule, obviously. Lots of people moan online, including senior executives from big companies and the agency people who hope to sell their services to big companies. If you choose to use social media to vent your spleen, remember that the people around you in your organization will see that as an example.

## WHAT YOU CAN DO RIGHT NOW

- Look at your existing HR and computer use policies and see how much they already cover that could apply to social media.

- Pick representatives from your legal and HR teams and task them with building a basic understanding of the social media issues in each of those areas. Send them to a conference, or find one of the many webinars on those topics.

- Do a Web search for "social media policies" (or go straight to socialmediagovernance.com). You'll most likely find some policies that are applicable to your company and can give you a head start on writing your own.

- Try to summarize your company's attitude to social media use in a clear, concise, and easily understood fashion.

CHAPTER **6**

# Staffing and Structuring

*Hell, there are no rules here. We're trying to accomplish something.*

—Thomas Edison

There's a group of people out there whom we refer to as "the self-appointed guardians of the purity of social media." Let's call them the SAGPOSMs. Or the sag possums.

The sag possums will tell you that social media needs to be free and unrestricted, across the enterprise, starting right now. They'll tell you that employees will figure out how to do social media by themselves and they'll inherently know not to say or do anything that could cause problems.

They'll tell you that social media should never be used to sell. They'll tell you that you can't measure the ROI of social media and that you shouldn't even try.

Oh, and they'll tell you that the best person to lead social media within your organization is your CEO.

The sag possums do not work for big companies.

The sag possums will also tell you that, because social media should be part of everybody's job, nobody should have a title like social media manager.

We agree with them. But we agree with them in maybe 2013.

When Dave applied for the social media manager job at SAS, he told people he didn't want to build a social media department. He wanted to work to integrate social media into all departments and identify and develop social media champions within each department. He told people that if he did his job right, it wouldn't be necessary within a few years.

Is that because of his own inherently self-destructive tendencies? No. It's because deep down he agrees with the sag possums that social media will become a part of everyone's job and that you can trust most employees to be smart and say and do the right things.

But you need a framework to get there.

For now, you need someone at your company immersed in social media. You need a digital native, or someone working like hell to catch up with the natives. You need someone who loves the idea of sitting on the couch on a Saturday night figuring out the differences between Foursquare and Gowalla and the differences between ping.fm and blip.fm.

You need to make that person a visible part of your social media efforts. Doing so sends the message that your company is serious about social media and values it enough to dedicate a resource to it.

Most important, you need that person to help you figure out what you're going to do, who's going to do it, and how.

Here's the relevant part of the job description of the SAS social media manager:

> The SAS Social Media Manager is both internally and externally focused on developing and executing SAS' social media strategy and advocating for the external community. Externally, he or she identifies influential opportunities, engages regularly with SAS' audiences online and may be called upon to speak publicly as a thought-leader on SAS' social media strategy. This person anticipates the evolution of social media. Internally the Social Media Manager sets the tone, philosophy and strategy (including budget) for Web 2.0, gains appropriate buy-in, then communicates relentlessly. He or she monitors Web 2.0 activities across departments and geographies, guiding participants on integration and best

practices while encouraging successful participation. The Social Media Manager is obsessively focused on how results connect to corporate objectives, and is given the tools to measure those results.

## WHERE DOES IT LIVE?

Once you've made the decision to put someone in charge, you have to decide where that person sits. Again, social media touches every aspect of a company's operations, from employee communications, to sales and marketing, to customer service. In an ideal world, your organization would give you the resources to hire and train people in every corner of your organization to drive social media participation for their group. And if you work for a company that's giving you blanket permission to hire anyone you need, keep it to yourself, because the rest of us don't want to hear it.

In some ways this is where smaller companies have an advantage over larger companies. If you have 5 or 10 or 20 people in your company, you could work with them directly to make social media a part of all of their jobs. In a larger organization, that goal will take much longer to accomplish and, again, is one of the reasons you need someone in charge.

Where that person sits will depend in large part on your organization and how you're currently structured to deal with customers, prospects, and the media. In general, though, for most typical large enterprises, it makes sense for social media coordination to be done by the people who already know how to deal with those groups. In your company that might be called marketing communications, or external communications, or public relations.

Who are the people in your company who know what to do when a reporter calls on deadline at 4:00 p.m. on a Friday asking for a reaction to major news from a competitor? Who are the people who know what to do if someone says something negative about your product in an online consumer forum? Who are the people who know what to do if a customer calls and says, "I'm a teacher, I love your product and have used it with my students for 20 years. Can I have some T-shirts for them?"

In your company that may be one person or it may be a combination, but ask yourself who the people are who are best suited to deal with many different kinds of requests and comments and coordinate your internal response. That's where the social media coordinating function should live in your organization, because as soon as you start participating, you'll get every kind of question and comment you can imagine.

## HIRE OR DESIGNATE?

Some people will tell you it's easier to teach a social media–savvy new hire about your company than it is to teach someone in your company to embrace and use social media. That may well hold true for your company. Only you can decide how difficult it is to teach someone about your company and get them to the point of being able to speak on your behalf.

How big a challenge would it be if you were hiring a new corporate spokesperson? Would you be able to get him or her up to speed in a few weeks?

The other side of that coin is reflected in the debate over Pizza Hut hiring a "twintern" (Twitter intern) in 2009 to tweet for them. The move drew criticism from some social media professionals, who thought it showed an insufficient respect for the value of social media to a brand's message. How can someone tweet for you, they argued, if they don't have a core knowledge of your company and its values?

If you're lucky, that question answered itself instantly. You might be thinking "That's easy. We'd put Sally in charge. She already has a blog and a Twitter account and has been coming to staff meetings for months showing us how our competitors are using social media and suggesting ideas for what we can do." If the answer is immediately clear to you, go with it.

If you choose to hire someone, be careful to define what you're looking for and what qualifications that person should have.

At this point in the social media world, there are many more self-proclaimed social media experts out there than actual experts. Every day people are gaining practical expertise in social media marketing and communications, but there is still a limited supply of people who have created and implemented social media strategies and tactics for companies.

If you post an ad for a social media manager or marketing specialist, you'll get a wide range of responses, and a lot will be from people who really want to learn to do the job but aren't necessarily qualified to do it yet.

The answer can be hard or simple, and there are lots of blog posts out there on the topic (search for the phrase "social media snake oil," and you'll find quite a few). In essence it's no different from hiring for any job: You'll need a clear understanding of your requirements that will let you find the person who matches them. The difference here is in the verification. You'll need to ask tougher questions and ask for more examples in order to feel comfortable that an applicant really knows the tools and techniques.

## HOW DO YOU STRUCTURE FOR SOCIAL MEDIA?

Jeremiah Owyang of Altimeter Group has done more work than just about anybody to figure out how companies should structure their social media activities. Jeremiah ran the social media program at Hitachi Data Systems from 2005 to 2007, then worked at Forrester Research as an analyst before joining Altimeter. He defines two primary types of role for social media professionals within organizations: social strategists and community managers.

### Social Strategist

The social strategist is responsible for the overall social media program within a company, including the ROI. This role is primarily focused internally on the programs, budget, and resources. Depending on the size of the organization and how it's structured, there may be more than one strategist.

Jeanette Gibson from Cisco, Zena Weist from H&R Block, Nichole Kelly from CareOne, and Bert DuMars from Newell Rubbermaid—all of whom you will meet in subsequent chapters—can be described as social strategists.

## Community Manager

The community manager is a customer-facing role, designed to be the face of a company in social media and build trust with customers. This role is externally focused. He or she is the community evangelist and advocate. Companies may have dozens of community managers.

Lionel Menchaca at Dell, whom you might know better by his Twitter handle @LionelatDell, is a good example of a community manager.

Jeremiah also describes several models organizations can employ: centralized, organic, hub and spoke, multiple hub and spoke or "dandelion," and holistic or "honeycomb."

### Centralized Model

In a centralized model, one department controls all efforts. Typically, corporate communications says "We own social media and it all comes through us." Jeremiah cites Scott Monty, Ford's head of social media, as an example of a strong central social media leader from the corporate communications department who does a good job of representing the company's brand in social media.

The risk of the centralized model is that the message may not look as authentic to the market. The tendency in this model, Jeremiah warns, may be to take the lazy route, for instance, rehashing press releases as blog posts.

"The upside of the centralized model is consistency," he adds. "If one department, skilled in creating corporate messaging, is responsible for the message in social media, you can be comfortably certain it will be on point and representative of the organization's goals."

### Organic Model

In an organic model, the dots may not all be connected. This is often the way social media participation develops in the absence of strong leadership. Social media bubbles up from all corners of the company, and it tends to look very authentic to outside observers. (Because it is.)

"The downside is you have an inconsistent customer experience," Jeremiah says, "and one side of the company doesn't know what the other side is doing. They may be deploying inconsistent systems that will create a long-term mess for marketing and IT."

Companies traditionally move out of this into another type of model, Jeremiah says.

### Hub-and-Spoke Model

Typically, there is a cross-functional team, often led by someone in marketing, Web marketing, or external communications. This team serves as the hub and engages business units, product teams, or geographies as spokes. The goal is to make sure everyone can do what they need to do, with the consistency of a central hub setting rules, best practices, and procedures. This approach can be resource-heavy, Jeremiah says. "The downside is you need dedicated resources, executive support, and funding. This model requires an investment."

### Multiple Hub-and-Spoke, or "Dandelion," Model

The hub-and-spoke model can scale. In larger enterprises you may find more than one.

"In the largest companies and multinationals," Jeremiah says, "we see multiple hub and spokes within product units and geographies. The goal is to ensure each individual hub and spoke is empowered, and supports corporate messaging and branding."

### Holistic, or "Honeycomb," Model

Jeremiah has seen the holistic model deployed in only a few companies. Each employee is empowered to participate in social media. There is little or no central control, but all the resources, planning, and procedures are designed to support the employees. Not every company can do this, Jeremiah warns, especially companies in regulated industries.

## HOW ONE ORGANIZATION PULLS IT TOGETHER

Zena Weist from H&R Block says her company has built on the hub-and-spoke model and modified it somewhat. She calls it a "revolving hub and spoke." Different members of the extended team may find themselves jumping in to take the hub role, depending on what's going on. We'll let Zena describe how it works.

> If we're having an issue with an office, HR is in the center. If there's a marketing issue, then marketing is driving it. The social media team pops in and out of the hub role depending on who is driving the issue and we pop off as someone helping to drive it. Who's in the hub depends on what the objective is.

The way Zena has staffed her team provides a smart blueprint for larger organizations hoping to integrate social media into their operations. The structure H&R Block has chosen takes into account the different roles required to address the various functions the social media department needs to address.

First, they have a strategist, who manages their social media presences that aren't part of HRBlock.com: Twitter, Facebook, YouTube, Twitter, forums, and interactions with the Yahoo! Answers message board. The strategist also handles the vendor relationships with those channels.

They have a community manager, who manages their Get It Right community of tax professionals who regularly answer tax questions online. This manager also works closely with the tax professionals who contribute to that community, managing all of the content the community shares and making sure they have an integrated communications strategy with the corporate communications team.

Their business analyst, according to Zena, is the "big-ears guy," who monitors the data that comes in through the monitoring platform and optimizes the algorithm, making sure they're following the conversations and gleaning the data that's most useful to them.

A project manager helps pull it all together and makes sure they're responding in the best possible way in all the channels they address.

## OUTSOURCING THE ROLES

Depending on the size of your company and how you like to do things, you may want to outsource these services rather than hire or train your own team. Or outsourcing may be an interim strategy while you're learning the ropes and deciding what organizational structure you'd like to implement.

You may have already been approached by agencies that want your social media business. Perhaps you work with an advertising firm or PR agency of record that is expanding to include social media services. Just as you need to be careful when hiring a social media practitioner for your company, be careful when selecting a social media agency. This is a brave new world, and there are as many charlatans out there (and well-intentioned neophytes) as there are experienced agencies with a track record of success. Maybe more.

The most important thing to consider is that you must be authentic and transparent. If you hire someone to pretend to be you, you will be found out, and your customers will not appreciate it. Any hint of deception in social media is treated harshly by the social media world. In the eyes of some, there is no greater sin than "sock puppetry," the practice of creating a fake identity to say good things about yourself online.

You can outsource many of the functions of a social media strategist and some of those of a community manager without breaking the unwritten rules. Later on you'll read about monitoring, measurement, and analytics, and those are all valid areas for outsourcing. Rather than develop an in-house listening and response apparatus and a process for analyzing the data you receive from social media, you might choose to let someone else do it for you.

Likewise, there are quite a few agencies that would be more than happy to help you create and implement a social media strategy for your company. This can be a very effective way to get started, providing you work with the right people.

Be careful when hiring consultants. Ask for references. Ask for results. Be clear about what you want. Show the same due diligence you would if your company were hiring an attorney or an accountant. And be cognizant of the fact that there are not a heck of a lot of people out there yet with a tremendous amount of experience in this field. The few agencies that do know what they're doing are preceded by their reputation.

Charlene Li of Altimeter offers some additional advice for selecting an agency.

It's important to be able to see and understand if they actually focus on relationships or campaigns, Charlene says. Lot of agencies know how to put up static Facebook splash pages, but they may not know how to interact.

Ask them to tell you when they've failed at social media and what they've learned. Charlene advises only hiring agencies that have "scars." Those that are willing to share the results of their mistakes and what they've learned will be more successful.

## WHAT YOU CAN DO RIGHT NOW

- Pick someone to lead your social media charge. If somebody doesn't immediately come to mind when you read that sentence, ask your department heads whom they think of.

- Give some thought to the structuring model that works best for your company. Are you small enough or centralized enough to have social media live in one group? Or do you need to create hubs and spokes?

- Decide if you want to bring it in house to start or to outsource to a social media agency.

# CHAPTER 7

# Listening, Measurement, Analytics, and ROI

*However beautiful the strategy, you should occasionally look at the results.*

—Winston Churchill

One of the key pieces of advice that Chris Brogan, president of New Marketing Labs, offers to companies (or anyone) getting started in social media is "Grow bigger ears." This is a maxim repeated over and over again in a variety of different ways: Listen before you talk. Join the conversation. Social media is a cocktail party.

The reason so many people talk about it is that it's right. The most important thing your company can do when getting started in social media is listen and learn. Hear what people are already saying about you, what channels they're saying it in, and the ways people communicate in those channels.

Unfortunately, there's no shortcut for this. You will not derive anything of value from social media if you are primarily concerned with broadcasting your message. If you can't accept that, put down this book and move on.

If you're still here, we'll talk about the different types of monitoring and measurement activity you can engage in to get some real value and build up to a model for measuring social media return on investment (ROI).

## A SIMPLE LISTENING FRAMEWORK

Listening is even more important in social media than talking. Your customers and prospects are sharing information daily about their business challenges, and you need to listen. There are lots of ways that you can take advantage of that information, but let's start with a simple listening framework.

You can create a simple dashboard to follow your areas of professional interest using free tools, most of them from Google:

- Create a Google account. You can use any email you want. You don't have to have a Gmail address.
- Set up a Google Reader account to aggregate RSS feeds. (Google has created an excellent video on YouTube that explains how to do this.)
- Create Google Alerts for key search terms and topics in your industry. You can receive them by email in your inbox or as a feed to Google Reader.
- Set up Google Blog Searches for the same terms. You can have those results sent to your Google Reader. If you'd like your Google Blog Search results sent via email, you can include "Blogs" as a category when setting up your Google Alerts.
- Perform searches in Twitter for the same terms, create an RSS feed from those searches, and follow the RSS feed in Google Reader.

If you're the kind of person who likes to tinker with Web tools, you can set up all of these feeds (and lots more) to create your own social media listening dashboard using freely available tools. iGoogle is a good one that will tie easily into all of your Google accounts. The easiest way to find any Google tool just referenced? Google it.

## FIRST, A WORD FROM THE MEASUREMENT QUEEN

We would be something more than remiss if we had a chapter about social media monitoring, measurement, analytics, and ROI and failed to mention Katie Delahaye Paine, "the Measurement Queen." Katie has consistently been one of the strongest and most effective voices in the social media world reminding us that none of this matters if it can't be measured. Her "Yes We Can Measure Social Media" stickers adorn the lid of many an influencer's laptop.

Katie has a clear answer to the question "How do you define social media ROI?"

> The first thing you have to do is define what the "R" is that you want to measure. What's the benefit to your company? Are you going to save money or bring money in? The "I" is the investment, and you need to be realistic about what that investment is. It is not free. It takes someone's time. Whether you're paying an agency or someone in house, it still costs money. And increasingly, social media outlets are looking for the revenue model, so costs associated with activities on Facebook, Twitter and the like are only going to go up.

> For most companies ROI falls into one of three categories. You're either going to save money because you're not going to have to do other things that cost money. You're going to bring in revenue through leads or lower cost of customer acquisition. Or you're going to bring in sales or grow market share by changing your perceptions or your relationships or your reputation.

What are the first things a marketing department should do to measure the effectiveness of its social media efforts? Katie says you need three basic components.

> You need to know what people are saying about you, what they are thinking about you and ultimately what they are doing to interact with your brand. Perhaps the

first thing you need to do is begin listening to what the marketplace is saying about you, your marketplace and your competition. That piece is all about collecting data from all the various channels in which your brand is being discussed.

Second, you need an ongoing mechanism to understand and ultimately measure the perceptions in the marketplace. If you're not already doing annual reputation or relationship surveys, you should be listening to the conversations to determine how the marketplace is positioning your brand or products. You also need some way to see if people trust you, are satisfied with the relationship, are committed and want you to succeed. In an ideal world, this analysis, whether done by survey or intensive content analysis of the conversations, should be done at least every six months.

Finally, you need some form of Web analytics that tells you what actions people are taking on your website or blog as a result of your social media activities. If you don't have the ability to look at the increase in repeat visitors, unique visitors, people who come back to your site for a second time—all those signs that people are being engaged in your site or your brand—you don't really know how well you're doing. In this era of "drive by flaming" and overwhelming inundation of data and messages, measuring engagement is a way to determine whether you are having a dialog, or just yelling ever more loudly. Are you establishing a relationship, or just accumulating casual "likes"? Because ultimately, an organization's relationships are what will differentiate it from everyone else.

## "LISTEN, YES. BUT THINK BIGGER."

Nathan Gilliatt is principal of Social Target, a consulting firm that helps companies plan and implement listening strategies. Social Target also researches companies that provide software and services for monitoring and analyzing social media and publishes reports to help companies make informed purchase decisions. When you ask Nathan about the importance of listening, his response is simple.

> Listen, yes. But think bigger. Fundamentally, social media is an incredible source of information that is publicly available on the Internet, some of which is relevant to your business. What could you do if you could process all of the information available to you on the Internet?
>
> If you want to become active in the social media realm, listening is the first step that everyone recommends. And you do this so you do everything else right. On an individual level, this is how you learn how it works. You lurk before you post. By listening first, you learn the language and the social norms with the various communities you'll discover, and they're not all the same.
>
> Organizationally, you're learning the existing environment. Who is talking about you? Who are they, both individually and as a group? What are they like? Who are the influencers who talk about you the most, and who are they as people? What are they talking about? What are the topics over time and what are the topics today? Where are they talking about you, what sites or communities or discussion groups? Why are they talking about you? What's their motivation for saying these things? Are they customers, fans, or detractors? When? Is it episodic or an ongoing discussion?

Nathan defines five different types of conversations organizations should listen for:

1. Customers talking to you
2. People talking about you
3. People talking about your competitors
4. People talking about your customers, suppliers, and partners (which is particularly interesting for B2B)
5. People talking about your market without mentioning brand names

As for that last one, Nathan cites statistics from strategic planning consultancy MotiveQuest that say if you're monitoring solely based on a brand name, you're missing 70 to 95 percent of the conversation. Nathan elaborates:

> You monitor for customer service because your customers are in social media, and they're using it as a way to express themselves when there's a problem, to contact the company for a response or maybe just to vent. But customer complaints are happening in public, and if you're monitoring, there's an opportunity to deal with them.
>
> From a PR perspective, the same activity can warn you of problems before they get big and give you an opportunity to avert a crisis. That's the defensive view. Those are the easy uses to sell because they tap into the fear motivation, and it's not too hard to agree that we don't want bad things to happen.
>
> If we move to positive motivation, this is the first step toward engaging and being relevant to the online community relevant to the business, and building positive relationships.

## THE FIVE KINDS OF LISTENING

Nathan says that listening is the overarching metaphor, but he likes to stretch the term and give it a bigger meaning. Listening is a whole category of activities that start online and deliver information and metrics that feed whatever you need to do next.

Nathan breaks listening down into five types of activities: search, monitoring, alerting, measuring, and mining.

### Search

Search in Nathan's hierarchy is just what you think it is: using search engines like Google or Bing or social media–specific tools like Social Mention or Board Reader to find out what people are saying on a specific topic. He says:

> Even if you haven't done anything at all in social media, you can go right now to a search engine and type in your

company name to see what people are saying. You can use one of the social-media specific tools to focus in those channels.

## Monitoring

Monitoring means using automated methods to find and read new mentions, or in other words, search over time. Nathan sees a number of ways that can be done.

> Rather than running the searches time and again, it delivers the new results to you. This is what a lot of the products on the market do. There are free tools, you can build your own with RSS feeds from search engines, or you can spend money on tools that people have already put together.

## Alerting

Alerting is like monitoring, but the difference is that new search results come to you, through emails or other alerts, so that you don't have to go back to a monitoring screen or dashboard. Google Alerts is the best known, freely available alerting tool. But you can take it another step, says Nathan.

> Where it gets really interesting is when you have threshold-based alerts: Based on activity reaching some value, the system generates an alert. If there's a burst of discussion around a new topic, for instance, or if one of your measured values suddenly spikes. If there's suddenly a burst of negative sentiment in the discussion around your brand, the system will send you an alert.

## Measuring

Measuring adds a quantitative element to monitoring. When you're measuring, you're aggregating data and generating numbers, which hopefully will mean something. Nathan says most social media metrics are pretty straightforward.

> The usual metrics you see based on social media activity
> are things like volume or number of items that match a
> query; sentiment, whether people are saying things good
> or bad; and most common topics.

Common metrics are volume, sentiment, topics, and sources, Nathan says. Dealing with sources brings up the notion of analyzing the influence of the people talking about you online.

Less common metrics include demographics, location, language, and outbound links (the links people are sharing in the conversations you're tracking).

## Mining

The distinction between measuring and mining, according to Nathan, can be arbitrary.

> Measuring is an ongoing practice where you're
> generating metrics you'll use to manage the business.
> Mining is more of a research activity and the output is
> more of a research product. It's looking at archival data
> and answering a research question, as opposed to
> generating numbers you'll compare quarter to quarter.

In the enterprise, the big difference may be in who is doing it and what their job is.

An organization might use mining for due diligence when scouting business partners, competitor research, or exploring scenarios for potential new business. Mining is the practice of looking for potential answers to business questions.

Where measurement becomes a routine capability, especially in a marketing context, mining is strategic. It's using publicly available data to answer strategic business questions.

If you want to do defensive keyword monitoring to head off complaints about your product, Nathan, says, that's good, but it's just one of several important listening activities. No one of these is the right answer. These are among the many things you need to think about.

> When you're tempted to fixate on one use, the model
> reminds you there are other things you might be doing.

> If you're doing monitoring, good for you. Have you considered measuring? If you're doing measuring, good for you. Have you considered mining?

How do you decide what is right for your organization?

> The mantra in the social media crowd is "It's not about the technology, it's about the people," which is correct, if you're talking about marketing strategy and connecting with consumers in these new spaces.

> When you're making a decision about what tools to bring in to support your listening strategies, it's entirely about technology. The way you make a technology decision is based on objectives, requirements and capabilities, in that order.

Dozens of software products and services on the market offer varying functionality. Some are merely listening tools; others offer more in-depth analytics. The prices range from free to tens of thousands of dollars. You need to do your research before you can make an informed buying decision. (And since Nathan was nice enough to give us so much valuable information for this book, we'll point out that Social Target publishes reports that can help with that.)

He offers a final piece of advice.

> Before you buy software or specialized listening services, you have to know your objectives. What are you trying to accomplish? Given the objectives, what do you need to accomplish them in your specific environment—not just the specifics of the software, but of your organization? Once you understand your requirements, then you can evaluate the capabilities of the software and services on the market.

## WHAT IS SOCIAL MEDIA ANALYTICS?

If you're familiar with the concept of business analytics, you know that it is the process of delivering insights gleaned from data about customers, suppliers, operations, and performance, giving organizations the power to solve complex business problems and make better decisions.

Social media analytics is a comparatively new term, but it's based on the principles of business analytics: If you can sort through all the information that your customers, prospects, and influencers are saying about you and analyze it based on your business objectives, you can use social media to make better decisions and sell more products.

John Bastone is product marketing manager for SAS Social Media Analytics, an enterprise social media software solution introduced in April 2010. John gets excited when he thinks about the possibilities of sifting through all that unstructured data out there in the form of tweets and updates and posts and coming out the other side with intelligence that will affect the bottom line.

Businesspeople understand analyzing numbers, John says, but how do you analyze a conversation?

> The reality is you can get a lot of actionable intelligence from digital conversations. Take Apple, for instance. David Pogue of the *New York Times* talks a lot about Apple, and reviews their products as soon as he can get his hands on them. David offers an intelligent and humorous perspective on the tech industry, has nearly a million and a half followers on Twitter, plus the people who read his blog, watch his videos, and find him in other venues for his insights. That's called influence. It's based on numbers and it can be calculated.
>
> Another key factor is sentiment analysis. For instance, if Apple were to look at Cnet.com over a specific period of time and pull out all the negative iPhone reviews, they might see that 55 percent specifically mention AT&T's "weak signal." Or that when Steve Jobs offered up his "Thoughts on Flash" in April 2010, 65 percent of the comments on professional media sites worldwide agreed with his point of view that Flash had technical drawbacks compelling enough to look ahead to HTML5 as a new standard for multimedia content. Those are both examples of sentiment analysis.

Sentiment analysis is not the same thing as social media analytics. Social media analytics brings it all together. John recommends an approach to social media analytics that consists of three core capabilities: listening, leveraging, and engaging. These are words you'll read often in this book, but social media analytics puts them in a slightly different, more specific context.

Listening is the first step, but just like Nathan Gilliatt, John says you need to do more than just listen. You need to listen critically, to help you understand if what you're hearing is accurate and relevant to your business.

> You have to categorize the conversations to align with the way you run your business. If you manage a brand, you want to know people's overall perception of the company. If you manage quality, you want to know what's breaking and making people mad.

> Technologies that enable critical listening include Web crawlers that can download relevant posts from key sites and word taxonomies which map key terms extracted from the textual data to the topics businesses need to track.

Listening tells you what people are saying, John says, but to leverage it, you need to understand *how* it is being said.

> Take a major hotel chain as an example. Listening will tell them that their customers talk about them on sites like Priceline.com. But that knowledge in and of itself doesn't do you any good unless you know what they're saying. Do they think check-in takes too long? Do they think the rooms are clean?

The people in your organization monitoring that information will appreciate being able to see the way sentiment changes over time—even minute by minute throughout the course of the day. A visual representation of the data can form the basis of a social media listening post or control center.

As the reach and impact of social networking continues to grow, it will be more and more important for organizations to be able to recognize trends and respond right away—and not just in crisis situations.

The final step in taking advantage of social media analytics, says John, is engagement. Once again, gathering the data, identifying the influencers, and seeing what people are saying about you doesn't mean anything unless you act on the information.

> You have to engage with the customers who are taking the time to talk about you online. And you have to close the loop inside your own organization. How can you use that information to improve your internal processes? Follow-up and follow-through are just as important in social media as they are in the real world.

If you're just getting started, John's advice is not to try to attack all three phases of social media analytics at once.

> Start with listening. Ask yourself what you're doing to help your company refine this reservoir of information into something that will actually move the needle. If you acknowledge how important social media is to your business without having a plan of action to take advantage of it, you're no better off than the companies with their heads in the sand who are ignoring social media altogether.

## CAREONE'S MEASUREMENT MODEL

CareOne Services Inc. is a debt relief company formed in 2002 to provide consumers with multiple solutions to complex money issues. Social Media Director Nichole Kelly and her team have blazed new trails with a variety of successful social media efforts to reach people who can benefit from their services. CareOne's leadership supports Nichole's approach. Even so, as we've said before, the bottom line is the bottom line. Nichole does a great job of defining the need:

> You still have to be able to tie your social media activities into something your executive team cares about. They care about acquisition and retention. You can use social media to generate brand awareness, but if you can't tie brand awareness into a sales funnel, it's really hard to get funding. At the end of the day, everything we do is tracked down to the sales funnel, and that's how we present it.
>
> We spend a lot of money every year on advertising. I have a budget that's a fraction of that. We're testing everything. We need to prove how it affects the bottom

line, so we can get the funding to do the cool stuff we know we should be doing.

Nichole is one of the smart enterprise social media practitioners who has figured out that you can't measure the ROI of social media without clearly defining your goals and breaking them down into discrete chunks. Doing this can sound like an insurmountable challenge if you're just getting started, but remember, here's the good news: You already know how to measure the success of your sales and marketing efforts. (You do, don't you? Someone in your organization is tracking the effectiveness of your email marketing campaigns, your online and traditional advertising, and your Website, right?) You need to do the work to integrate your social media sales and marketing activities with your other sales and marketing activities, Nichole says.

> We wanted to be able to tie our social media tracking
> and measurement into our existing systems. We use
> an in-house campaign manager tool that creates unique
> URLs for campaigns and short URLs we can use in
> social media channels. The system sets cookies when
> people visit our site, so we can see when they visited,
> where they went to after they left, and when they
> came back.

(You may have just read that paragraph while nodding in silent comprehension. Or it may have sounded vaguely familiar. Or it may have sounded like total gibberish. In any case, if you're working for an enterprise-level organization, there's someone in your Web or IT department who will know exactly what Nichole is talking about.)

Nichole has defined a sales funnel with five categories: exposure, influence, engagement, action/conversion, and retention. She has developed metrics for each of these categories. As she says on her blog at www.nicholekelly.com:

> Just remember that social media is just a tool in your
> marketing tool kit. If you measure social media using
> some of the same measurements you've always used,
> it will start to make sense and be easier to justify
> your efforts.

| Category | Metrics |
|---|---|
| Exposure | Visits to your Website<br>Views of your pages and posts<br>Number of Twitter followers<br>Number of fans/"likers" of your Facebook page<br>Number of subscribers to your blog<br>Brand mentions in traditional and social media |
| Influence | **Share of voice:** How much of the conversation about your field in social media is about your brand?<br>**Sentiment:** Are people saying good or bad things about you?<br>**Top influencers:** Are influential people talking about you? |
| Engagement | The number of clicks on your links<br>How often people retweet what you say on Twitter<br>How often people reply to you on Twitter<br>How many direct messages you get on Twitter<br>How many times people post something on your Facebook wall<br>The number of comments on your blog<br>How often people share your content with their networks |
| Action/<br>Conversion | Content downloads<br>Webinar attendance<br>Lead generation forms<br>Pitches/proposals<br>Purchase |
| Retention | Customer retention as tracked by your existing metrics |

If you were looking for a simple formula, we're sorry. But how often in your experience does a simple formula, applied to a large problem, deliver usable data? It will take time, effort, and understanding of the various channels to work social media metrics into your existing tracking and measurement systems. But when you are done, you will have something of real value—something no "online ROI calculator" or a consultant offering a quick fix can provide.

## NOT A SIMPLE FORMULA, BUT A FORMULA NONETHELESS

If you're looking for a way to break down your social media efforts to a dollar amount for each activity, you can do that. It won't be simple, but if you do the work to set it up, you can get bottom line numbers.

One of the earliest debates in the social media world centered around the idea of whether you could measure the ROI of social media. Some people responded with questions like "What's the ROI of picking up the phone? What's the ROI of taking a customer out to play golf?" They used those arguments to say that it wasn't necessary to be able to track the ROI of your social media efforts. They argued that we should be talking not about return on investment but about "return on engagement" or "return on influence."

We don't think those people worked for big companies. For most corporate sales and marketing people, the only measure that matters is how much stuff you sell compared to how much money you spent to sell it.

As the field of enterprise social media has grown, not only have more people seen its value, but more people have realized we need ways to measure the success of our efforts and whether they're worth the money and people power. In other words, the ROI.

Remember first of all that social media is not a strategy in itself. It's a set of tools and a philosophy of communication. Your social media efforts need to support your existing goals, objectives, and strategies in order to be successful. And in order to be measurable.

You have to know what you're trying to achieve before you can measure it or see if it's working. If your goal is to build your company's reputation, that will drive a significantly different set of measures than if your goal is to sell more left-handed flange arrestors.

If your goal is to sell more products, then you have a clear objective you can work toward measuring. The good news: You probably have all the data you need in house already. It's just a matter of putting it together.

Christopher S. Penn, vice president of strategy and innovation for email service provider Blue Sky Factory, is often referred to as a "marketing ninja," not just because of his interest and proficiency in the martial arts but because he has a way of pinpointing the confusion that sometimes accompanies social media marketing and cutting through it like a warm *katana* through butter.

He has outlined an approach for calculating social media ROI that is as simple as it is brilliant (or possibly even cunning). Chris has kindly included worksheets to help you calculate all of these formulas on the Blue Sky Factory Website at www.blueskyfactory.com.

There are a lot of things you can measure in marketing, and a lot of ways to measure them, Chris says. There are two types of metrics: diagnostic and objective. Diagnostic metrics are indicators that tell you which way things are going. Objective measures show the actual results of what you want to achieve. Here's how Chris describes it:

> Diagnostic measures tell you how the trip is going. Objective measures tell you when you get there. Return on investment is very much an objective goal.

> Diagnostic metrics help us understand our sales and marketing processes, but aren't the bottom-line goal. Diagnostic metrics include the traffic to your Website, the number of Twitter followers you may have, the number of comments to your blog, the number of times people click on your online ads and the number of qualified leads that come into your funnel.

> They're important but they're not the bottom-line truth. Don't disregard them, but don't measure your ROI by them. Where we tend to go wrong with diagnostic metrics is treating them like end goals.

> If the end goal of your workout is to see a certain number of miles on the readout on your treadmill, you can get there by putting your cat on the treadmill. But you've lost sight of the true end goal, which is to lose weight.

Chris demystifies the concept of ROI by breaking it down into a simple formula:

$$\frac{Earned - Spent}{Spent} = ROI$$

The amount of money you earned, minus the amount of money you spent, divided by the amount of money you spent equals your return on investment. "If you're trying to measure financial performance," Chris says, "this is the only measure that matters."

Where ROI can get messy, Chris says, is in calculating the amount of money spent.

> The amount of money earned is easy. That's just money in the door. Calculating your spend has to take into account a lot of factors, including time spent. How might you calculate your time spent as a dollar value?

First, you need to understand the dollar value of the time spent. If you're doing the work yourself, then you need to know your hourly rate. If you're a consultant, you know that number already. If you earn a regular salary, then it's just a matter of simple math to figure out how much you earn per hour: your annual salary divided by 2,080, the number of working hours in a standard year.

If you're looking at the value of time spent by a company or organization, then obviously you're looking at the hourly rate, or hourly rate equivalent, of all the team members involved. If you know the hourly rate and the time the team spent on a project, you know what the project cost you.

And if you know what your campaign cost compared to how much you earned, then you can figure your ROI.

$$\frac{\text{Total Earned} - \text{Total Spent}}{\text{Total Spent}} = \text{ROI}$$

These formulas work equally well for pay-per-click advertising on the Web, email marketing campaigns, Twitter campaigns, or in fact any campaign where you can calculate the time you spent compared to what you earned.

People like to say that social media is free, but you need to take into account the time you spend on a campaign. Chris shares actual numbers from a Twitter campaign as an example. The campaign brought in leads that led to $750 worth of business. There was no actual out-of-pocket cost for using Twitter, so the money spent was $0. But the marketer calculated he spent an entire 40-hour week on the campaign at an effective hourly rate of $24.04, for a total cost of $961.60. In other words, a 22 percent negative return. For every dollar spent on that campaign, the marketer effectively lost 22 cents when he included the value of his time.

Simple, yes, but Chris suggests another, more useful metric that he calls net earnings per lead, or EPL. That formula looks like this:

$$\frac{\text{Earned} - \text{Spent}}{\text{Number of Leads}} = \text{EPL}$$

"Net earnings per lead is a better tactical number than pure ROI," Chris says, since it gives you a better comparison against your other marketing expenditures.

Once you've calculated your net earnings per lead for each channel, you can then calculate your average earnings per lead for all your channels, which is an even more useful standard of comparison. Chris advises including everything that's working that (has a positive ROI) and everything that might not be working that you're committed to doing. For instance, if Twitter isn't returning for you but you're committed to sticking with it because you feel it has growth potential, include it in your overall average.

Average net earnings per lead, Chris says, helps you understand when you might be losing money on marketing tactics. Obviously, you would consider decreasing (possibly to zero) the amount of time and resources spent on the channels that aren't earning you a profit.

In the end, Chris advises, none of these metrics means anything unless you act on them. Do the work to understand the numbers and then use that data to make the practical business decisions about your social media activities.

# WHAT YOU CAN DO RIGHT NOW

- Sign up for a Google account if you don't already have one.
- Set up Google Reader.
- Create Google Alerts for your name, your company name, the names of your products, your competitors, and key search terms and topics in your industry.
- Set up Google Blog Searches for the same terms.
- Perform searches in Twitter for the same terms, create an RSS feed from those searches, and follow the RSS feed in Google Reader.
- Perform keyword searches on YouTube and see who's posting videos related to your industry.
- Find the groups on Facebook and LinkedIn where people are talking about your company, your products, your competitors, and your industry.
- Start off any new social media activity by asking "What do we want to accomplish, and how will we know if we've accomplished it?"

# CHAPTER 8

# The Keys to Success in Social Media

*Once you shift your focus from yourself to others and extend your concern to others, this will have the immediate effect of opening up your life and helping you to reach out. The practice of cultivating altruism has a beneficial effect not only from a religious point of view but also from a mundane point of view; not only for long-term spiritual development but even in terms of immediate rewards.*

—The Dalai Lama, via Facebook

## IT'S DIFFICULT IN ITS SIMPLICITY

While successful social media strategy and practice is a large topic that occupies the time of hundreds of bloggers, consultants, and "experts" on a daily basis, there are some fundamental principles of success in using social media for business purposes.

These principles permeate the examples you'll read in this book. Some of them may be easy to accept; some may be more difficult. We recognize that we're asking you to accept two major ideas that seem like they might be contradictory, but if you can keep both of these in your head at the same time, you're well on your way to succeeding:

1. **Social media is driving the biggest revolution in the way companies communicate since the introduction of the World Wide Web.** It will eventually touch—and change—everything you do.

2. **If you're a successful businessperson, you already understand the fundamental truths that social media is built on.** And if you already understand how your business works and where you want to go, putting social media to work in support of your existing goals and objectives is just a matter of doing the hard work to understand the points of integration.

If we haven't already given you a headache, here are what we consider to be the five keys to success in social media:

1. **Be real.** Don't try to pretend you're someone you're not, because people will find you out and you will destroy your credibility. Be as open and transparent as you can be, based on the realities of your company and your business. Admit it when you make mistakes. Be honest with people, and make a genuine effort to be a valuable member of the online community.

2. **Be relevant.** If you want people to follow your social media activities, you need to gear your efforts toward what your audience cares about, not what you care about. If all you share are marketing messages about your company, then the only people you will reach will be other marketers from your company, a few hard-core devotees, and your competitors.

3. **Be practical.** Social media is a set of tools and a philosophy of communication, not a strategy in itself. Your social media activities need to be tied directly to supporting your established campaigns, goals, and objectives. Before you begin a social media activity, decide what the objective is and how you will measure its success.

4. **Be patient.** Social media is not a quick fix. Establishing a presence in social media takes time. You need to build a following, whether you're starting a blog, a YouTube channel, a Facebook fan page, or a Twitter feed.

5. **Be active.** Social media is about community, sharing, and immediacy. If you want to develop a social media presence, you need to contribute on a regular basis and keep your content fresh.

Now let's look at the ways successful companies are putting these principles into action and what you can do to make them work for your business.

## FINDING THE TIME TO DO IT

One of the biggest concerns people (and managers) have when they think about using social media for business is how to add something new to an already full plate. We have yet to run across anyone in the modern business world who will say "I've got nothing better to do with my time. What else have you got for me?" (Or at least no one who will admit it.) "I don't have time" is the biggest single objection we've heard when talking to executives and managers about participating in social media.

In general, people seem to be concerned about two things: keeping up with new communications channels and developing content for those channels. Neither challenge is easy, but neither is hard if you break each down into its component parts and think about what you're already doing that you can repurpose and reuse.

Here's the good news: If you're working in an organization of any size, you are probably already creating tons of content that you can use: white papers, webinars, case studies, customer success stories, technical documentation, company newsletters, email content, and more. The hard part is creating the intellectual property that someone else will find interesting and valuable. Sharing it in social media is the easy part once you figure out how.

First, a caveat: As we've said before, social media is in part a new philosophy of communication. There's a reason the phrase "You have to join the conversation" has become overused in the context of social media to the point of becoming hackneyed: because it's true. The first commitment you need to make is to listen and learn, and learn to follow the standards and modes of behavior in the online channels you wish to join.

Next, you need to commit to becoming a valuable member of the community, not just a mouthpiece for your brand. Thinking about ways you can provide value and items of interest that have nothing to do with your company is even more important than thinking about how you can promote yourself. It's the only way people will pay attention to you and want you in their network.

So let's assume that if you've gotten this far in this book, you're on board with that idea, and ready to talk about content.

## A SIMPLE MODEL

Kirsten Watson is director of corporate marketing at Kinaxis, developers of on-demand supply chain management software. Kinaxis has learned a lot by building its Supply Chain Expert Community.

Kirsten spoke at a MarketingProfs conference about the way Kinaxis maximizes content for social media. It was such a clear and immediately understandable model, nearly everyone we have described it to finds it brilliant in its simplicity.

First of all, Kirsten's strategy is based on a solid understanding of the traffic to the Kinaxis Website. The company follows its Web analytics results closely to see what keywords people are searching that lead them to the Kinaxis site. Kirsten says search engine optimization (SEO) is key.

Kirsten's team creates an editorial calendar based on the top keywords it gets from its SEO analysis. Every month team members write a new white paper based on that keyword analysis, so they know it's a topic their site visitors care about. Then they use that content in nearly every way imaginable:

- The white paper becomes a series of blog posts.
- They interview the writer on video and post a talk about the topic on YouTube.

- The audio from the interview is turned into a podcast that is syndicated through iTunes.

- They create a PowerPoint presentation on the topic and post it to SlideShare, a free online service that allows people to post their own presentations and search for ones posted by others.

All of those pieces of content are posted and tagged with the appropriate keywords, so that someone searching for similar content on YouTube or iTunes or SlideShare is likely to find content from Kinaxis. It's a brilliant and simple strategy.

For anyone questioning whether they can create content for social media, the Kinaxis model should be inspiring. The results should inspire you as well. Kinaxis has seen a 2.7x increase in Web traffic to kinaxis.com, a 3.2x increase in conversions (measured as leads), a 5.3x increase in community traffic, and a 6x increase in membership. And it's seen double-digit growth in paid subscriptions to its RapidResponse software-as-a-service product.

## USING ALL YOUR CHANNELS

Here we are talking about Chris Brogan again, but his concept of outposts and home bases really does make a lot of sense when you're talking about how to feed content to all of your channels. Remember, the idea is that you want people to find your company in the places they frequently like to find information.

If someone loves Facebook and uses it all day long, wouldn't you like to be there if they search for your company? Likewise blogs, Twitter, and YouTube. They are all places where people hang out and, increasingly, search for business topics. Be there for them.

If your blog or your corporate Website is your home base, you can place your content there and share it out to your other channels. Facebook and LinkedIn both allow you to import RSS feeds, so your blog post can show up there.

Lots of people use Twitter to tell their followers when they've written a new blog post. In blog platforms like WordPress, you can even set up plug-ins that automatically send a tweet when you post.

When you post a video to YouTube, embed it in your blog. Send a tweet telling people you've posted a new video.

Corporate marketers and communicators have put together integrated marketing communications plans for years. Social media doesn't change the basic principle of integrating your channels to present a unified and consistent message. It's just a matter of figuring out the tools.

## NINE EASY WAYS TO WRITE A BLOG POST

Still not convinced you can create content to fuel your social media efforts? Here are some tips from Alison Bolen, SAS' editor of blogs and social content. She's a tireless champion of blogging and has helped turn many a skeptic into a dedicated blogger.

Alison's point mirrors the one we mentioned earlier: You are creating content every day that people would find useful and interesting if you would just put it out there in front of them. She offers nine ideas for how you can take what you've already written and turn it into a blog post. Yes, you: a blogger.

1. Go through your sent items on Friday. Pull out anything that's more than five paragraphs long and polish it into a blog post.

2. Go to search.twitter.com and search for two keywords. Write a three-paragraph post that responds to one or more of these tweets.

3. What are you consuming? Business books, other blogs, podcasts, TV shows—anything that you're finding especially useful and interesting? Tell people about it in two or three paragraphs.

4. Take 20 minutes at the end of the day and think about who you've talked to today and what you've learned. How can you summarize that into a 200-word post that others can learn from as well?

5. What did you explain to someone today that you've explained at least three times before? If you get asked often enough, others would probably love to hear the explanation too. Give it to them in a blog post.

6. What cool things are your customers doing? What have you learned from them lately? What innovative ways are they using your product or service? Can't talk about customers without approval? Maybe you can mention them anonymously. Give details, just not names.

7. What documents or presentations are you working on right now? Can you excerpt two or three paragraphs into a quick blog post to give readers a sneak peak?

8. What are you researching? What would you like to learn more about? Ask your readers to explain it to you. Or do a Twitter search on the topic and see what you find. Link to results and share your thoughts.

9. Read the blogs on your blog roll. Find at least one to comment on. Then copy your comment on your blog and expand on it slightly. Link back to original post.

Is the fact that it's a list of nine, not a top ten, bothering you? Okay, then:

10. Write a top ten list.

## WHAT YOU CAN DO RIGHT NOW

- Make a list of all the content your company creates on a regular basis.
- Make a list of all the communications channels, social media and otherwise, at your disposal.
- Create a matrix from those two lists, and see how many places you can share each piece of content.
- Look at all the content you create on a regular basis, from reports to emails. Still think you don't write enough to fill a blog? How about a tweet?

# PART
## III

---

# Putting Your Social Media Strategy to Work

This author (Dave) has spent a lot of time talking to very smart marketers, communicators, salespeople, and other professionals about integrating social media into a corporate environment to support bottom-line goals and objectives. In 2008, the biggest question he faced was "Why?" By 2010, with a half-billion people on Facebook and seemingly every third article in the business press about Twitter, he wasn't being asked why quite as often. He was being asked "How?"

Even people who know and love social media tools can have a hard time articulating how they can and should be used for business. These are early days, similar to the dawn of the World Wide Web. Enterprise social media isn't in its infancy any longer, but it's hardly grown up, moved out, and coming home to do laundry. In short, we're still figuring it out.

Luckily, there are a lot of smart, imaginative, and level-headed pioneers out there who are not only blazing new trails but leaving a map for the rest of us to follow.

CHAPTER **9**

# Marketing

*Nothing draws a crowd like a crowd.*

—P. T. Barnum

At the time we are finishing up this book and getting ready to send it off to the publishers, there is a social media campaign that is getting a lot of attention. By the time you read this, people of the future, you may well be sick of it. By the time you read this, we will know what the bottom-line value of this campaign was to sales. But for now, the Old Spice campaign is the hottest thing to hit social media marketing since the last thing.

Built on the success of a TV commercial that debuted at Super Bowl XLIV and then went viral on YouTube, the integrated social media campaign stars shirtless ab merchant Isaiah Mustafa. Created by advertising agency Wieden + Kennedy, the social media campaign was built around dozens of personalized YouTube responses recorded by Mustafa in response to all kinds of people who mentioned Old Spice on Twitter and Facebook. And not just people with lots of followers like Ashton Kutcher and Alyssa Milano.

The campaign achieved staggering results, driving more than one million views on the first day, increasing Twitter followers by several thousand percent, shooting up the number of Facebook "likers" (nearly one million as of October 2010) and, most important, boosting sales more than 100 percent in the month after the campaign began.

Old Spice followed up quickly with a voice mail message genera-
tor, a Web-based tool that allowed fans to enter their own phone
number, select from a menu of options, and end up with a download-
able file they could use as their own outgoing message. So you could
have Mustafa's voice saying something like "The tall, accomplished
man you're calling can't come to the phone right now because they're
cracking walnuts with their man mind. But leave a message and
they'll return your call as soon as possible. I'm on a horse."

(That will be funny only if you've seen the ads. If you haven't,
trust us: It's funny.)

Why has this campaign gotten so much attention, and what can
marketers learn from it? For a start, Wieden + Kennedy defied one of
the accepted truths of social media marketing. If social media's effectiveness is built on one-to-one connections, some people argue, "It
doesn't scale." In other words, you can't make a personal connection
with people through broadcast means.

We agree with that. But Wieden + Kennedy *did* make it scale.
How? By being smart and working their butts (or abs) off.

Here's what Old Spice and Wieden + Kennedy did right:

1. The campaign demonstrated an understanding of the communities it was addressing. It was written in the right language. It
   even garnered positive responses to the video directed at the
   "anonymous" users of 4chan, an Internet site populated by
   people who love nothing more than poking holes in just about
   anything.

2. The campaign demonstrated an understanding of social media
   channels, what the individual characteristics of those channels
   were, and what benefits could be derived from each. It used
   Twitter, Facebook, YouTube, and Digg, the social news Website
   where people can promote stories they like. It knew what
   the value of each of those channels would be, and how to use
   them. How did Wieden + Kennedy know that? Through
   hard work and hiring people who know what they're talking
   about.

3. The campaign featured great content. Everybody wants their
   campaign to "go viral," and the Old Spice campaign demon-

strates once again what it takes to make that happen. The scripts for the videos are funny, edgy, and innovative.

4. The campaign featured great talent. Despite the previous description, Isaiah Mustafa is much more than a pretty torso. He's a talented comic actor with great timing and is apparently an ironman, considering he stood in a towel for a very long time, cranking out video after video. Isaiah was supported by a social media team and a group of writers who are obviously at the top of their game. Again, the videos are genuinely funny.

5. Finally, Old Spice knew when to quit. Rather than milking it to the point where people were sick of it, the campaign ended on a high note, ending the personalized video responses with a thank-you video to everyone. The comments to that video on YouTube are mostly along the lines of "Oh, no! You can't go!"

No doubt we will see a flood of imitators trying to duplicate Old Spice's formula. Many of those efforts will ring hollow. Inevitably, some will be downright embarrassing. I'm sure a lot of corporate marketers are looking at this and thinking "All you need to make a splash on the Web is a good gimmick."

Good marketers already know that breakthrough campaigns are built by smart people with great ideas, amazing content, and a solid understanding of their customers and the places they congregate, backed by intelligent execution.

Now let's take a look at a good marketer who has put all those principles to use in support of a brand you might not necessarily associate with the cutting edge.

## FROM STROLLERS TO SHARPIES

When you have products as diverse as permanent markers, food storage containers, and baby strollers, it might be hard to imagine how to apply a common social media marketing approach to all of them. Newell Rubbermaid has the answer: Focus on the communities around your products and help them tell their stories. Show your customers how real people use your products to make their lives easier and more enjoyable, and the products will sell themselves.

Bert DuMars is vice president of E-business and interactive marketing for Newell Rubbermaid, a century-old company that started out making curtain rods and grew to a global portfolio of brands, with 90 percent of American households having at least one of its products in their homes. Bert says his passion for social media and his confidence in its potential led him to his current position.

Corporations often find themselves blazing new trails, Bert says, "because someone steps up and says 'I'll take that on.' That's what I did."

Bert freely admits that, for brands, social media "is kind of scary." He recounts a football aphorism generally attributed to Woody Hayes:

> "There are three things that can happen when you throw a pass, and two of them are bad."

> Social media is the same way. It's very valuable to experiment. It allows you to try things on a small scale, so if you make a mistake it won't blow up.

When Bert first began to see social media's potential in 2007, Newell Rubbermaid's Graco brand of children's products had already taken its first tentative social media baby steps. Graco's marketing team thought social media could help reinvigorate the brand and help it better connect with expectant moms and parents.

Bert also recommends asking your community what it would like to hear from you. Early, face-to-face discussions with the mom bloggers Graco hoped to reach gave them great feedback. "They told us, 'Don't pound me over the head with information about your products. Talk to me about being a parent,'" Bert recalls.

With new parents on the team, Graco found it easy to speak authentically on its blog, "Heart to Heart." You could spend quite a bit of time on the Heart to Heart blog before you figured out it's run by a company with products to sell. There are first-person posts about bringing a baby home from the hospital for the first time, reader-submitted cute kid photos, and a how-to guide for soothing a newborn (most popular, we're guessing, between the hours of 3:00 and 5:00 a.m.)

Graco extends the reach of the blog through a Graco Baby Twitter stream (@GracoBaby) and a page on the popular photo-sharing site Flickr, which not only shares photos of Graco products but has even more cute kid pics, and photos submitted for contests. The Graco Baby YouTube video channel shows still even more cute kids, plus instructional videos on things like how to fold a stroller or install a car seat. (If you've ever tried to install a car seat yourself, we suspect you just had a moment there.)

Graco has adopted the same approach on the brand's Facebook page, which in mid-2010 had nearly 5,000 fans— people who have voluntarily chosen to receive news and information from Graco in their Facebook streams. Parents ask questions about Graco products and get answers from Graco customer service representatives as well as members of the community.

Graco creates a sense of community around its products by communicating with parents the way parents communicate with one another. The people who make up the Graco social media team have shown their consumers they are real people who share the same needs and desires. And as a result, the community has accepted them as people, not as a faceless corporation.

While it may be difficult to quantify a direct correlation between the blog and sales of Graco products, Bert points to one concrete example of how their commitment to the community resulted in a tangible benefit and helped turn a potential PR black eye into a positive.

Not too long ago, Graco recalled a stroller that had the potential to pinch a child's fingers in the hinge. Several children were hurt, and the mainstream media latched on to the story, says Bert.

> There were concerned parents trying to figure out if their stroller was involved and what they needed to do. We had a simple fix for the problem and we put it up on YouTube. We asked users to fill out a form, and we would send them the fix.

> The Graco Baby team engaged with parents through their social media channels, apologized, showed that they understood the parents' concerns and provided a solution.

> After three days, it wasn't just us responding, it was our
> community: moms telling other moms where to get the
> fix.

That kind of community support doesn't happen overnight, Bert advises. It can take years to build up. But it also answers the question "Will social media pay off for our company?" At a critical point for Graco, its engagement with the community paid off in spades.

## FROM THE NURSERY TO THE KITCHEN

Social media marketers for the Rubbermaid Consumer family of products learned a lot from Graco's experience. Faced with a challenge familiar to all marketing teams, they had to decide what they would get for the resources they expended. They started by defining their overall goal.

> Rubbermaid is a decades-old brand with high brand
> recognition, but what does it stand for? Most people will
> say trash cans and totes, but we wanted to reposition the
> brand around organization. We knew it would take time,
> but we also knew social media would be a great way to
> support the effort.

The Rubbermaid Consumer blog is called "Adventures in Organization." Now, that may not sound like a hot topic to you, but there are millions of consumers who are passionate about decluttering, as witnessed by the proliferation of TV shows designed to shame pack rats and disgust neat freaks.

The blog could easily have become a showcase for bins, but Rubbermaid took a smarter approach. It's not about the products, Bert says.

> It's about how to organize. How can we make it easier
> for our customers to organize their garages, their
> kitchens, their basements?

A random selection of blog posts from June 2010 includes a post about organizing a master closet, a first-person account of a cross-country move and the packing tips the author learned (with a few photos of items packed safely into Rubbermaid totes), and a Q&A with a professional organizer.

## SHARPIE, MEET LAMBORGHINI

Newell Rubbermaid's slogan for its extremely popular Sharpie permanent marketer is "Uncap what's inside," and the marker's many fans
have found amazing ways to demonstrate that their creative juices are
in no danger of running dry, smearing, or fading.

The company celebrates that creativity through its Sharpie
Uncapped brand community Website, which serves as a home base
for a gallery of photos of creative endeavors made with Sharpies and
links to the Sharpie blog, a Flickr photo page, and YouTube video
channel celebrating the many ways people use Sharpies.

> We want to uncap the creativity within everyone. We
> showcase our consumers and recognize them for their
> creativity. There are an infinite number of uses for
> Sharpie.

> We've had people on the blog who dye wigs with
> Sharpies. People who fix furniture, who fix their shoes.
> We highlighted a high school couple who decorated
> white outfits for their prom with Sharpies.

Artist Jona Cerwinske detailed a Lamborghini Gallardo with
Sharpie markers, covering nearly every inch of the car with intricate,
tattoo-like designs. The car is exhibited at auto shows. (It's worth
googling "Sharpie Gallardo" to see the pictures. We'll wait.)

But the brand's Facebook page may provide the boldest underline
to Sharpie's social media strategy. The Sharpie team uses Facebook as
another outlet to showcase the many uses people have for Sharpies,
events like music festivals that Sharpie fans are interested in, and also
the charitable endeavors the company supports.

In order to receive updates from Sharpie on Facebook, fans need
to click the "Like" button to opt in. At the time we're writing this,
Sharpie had more than 1 million fans. In the week between talking
to Bert and writing this, the number had increased by 2,000.

That's 1 million plus people who have said "I like Sharpie and I
want to read what you want to tell me, right here in my Facebook
stream among updates from my friends and family and colleagues and
people I knew in high school and had largely forgotten."

Think about the traditional advertising and marketing methods you've used. How much time, effort, and money did it take to reach 1 million people?

## BERT'S ADVICE

Bert's first piece of advice for any company getting started in social media is "Always start small, no matter how big the brand is." Try new things and learn from them, see the results and adjust accordingly. Don't be afraid to make mistakes, but they can be small mistakes.

Second, start by thinking in terms of building community, Bert suggests.

> Find the advocates who have passion for your brand, even if it's 10 or 100 or 1,000. Meet with them in person at least once. Let them get to know someone from the brand.

Throughout this book we say that social media needs to support your existing objectives. Bert agrees. What's the primary image you want to convey?

Think in terms of the themes you'll be covering. For Rubbermaid, it's organization. For Graco, it's parenting. For Sharpie, it's creativity.

If you can articulate your objectives and themes in simple terms, it will make it that much easier to find the right social media approach to support them.

Think in terms of the long-term benefit, Bert says. It takes time to build your social media presence. Resist the urge to listen to the snake oil salesmen who will sell you the social media equivalent of get-rich-quick schemes.

> Don't get frustrated. This is not a sprint. You're not going to build up a million followers overnight. Build it organically over time and you'll have a community that will support you and come to your aid.

Finally, it's vital to be a genuine member of the communities in which you participate. If you launch an insincere effort in social media, people will see right through you.

For any brand that's going to be out there, you have to figure out how you will show you care. A lot of people think brands—big, small or medium—are just out to make a buck. Building a community is about how to show that you care about your consumers. If you can't figure out how you're going to show you care, then I wouldn't go out there. Everyone talks about listening, but you need to listen, respond, and act.

## WHAT YOU CAN DO RIGHT NOW

- Think like your customers, and make a list of the issues most important to them, that keep them up at night and that bring them joy.
- Find the online communities where your customers congregate.
- Start looking for the people who are already passionate evangelists of your brand. Spend a lot of time listening to them before you say anything.
- Once you understand the communities they use and the way they communicate, start finding some genuine ways to show them you recognize and appreciate them.

# CHAPTER 10

# Social Media for B2B

*Profit in business comes from repeat customers, customers that boast about your project or service, and that bring friends with them.*

—W. Edwards Deming

When we talk about social media for sales and marketing, the first examples that often come to mind are in the business-to-consumer (B2C) space. In October 2010, Coca-Cola had almost 13 million fans on Facebook. (That number has more than doubled since we started writing this book.) Starbucks has more than 14 million. (Up from 8 million when we first looked.) That's a lot of caffeine lovers who like to show their affection for their favorite brown liquids.

But what about me? you ask. My company is business-to-business (B2B). We don't sell drinks, you say, we sell things in gray boxes with wires coming out of them that occasionally make a quiet bleeping noise. Why would anyone want to follow us on Twitter or Facebook or watch our videos?

Since you're already talking to yourself, ask yourself a question. When was the last time you settled down on a Saturday night in your favorite chair and thought, "I can't think of anything I'd rather do right now than read those product spec sheets I got from vendors"?

Whether we're talking about B2B or B2C, the Bs are all people, and people like to be engaged. They like to be entertained. They like to make connections with other people.

Jeffrey L. Cohen is a veteran digital marketer and social media marketing manager at Howard, Merrell and Partners, a Raleigh, North Carolina, strategic branding and advertising agency. He's also managing editor at SocialMediaB2B.com, a blog that chronicles the value B2B companies are finding in the social sphere.

> If you look at the basic characteristics of B2B sales, it's about relationships and the long sales cycle. Often B2B companies are selling complicated products, and more than one person is involved in the purchase decision. At its heart, social media is about connecting with people, providing value to them, and building a relationship.

> The first time a B2B salesperson makes a call, he's not selling yet. He's building a relationship and looking for ways to provide value. It may be as simple as providing a spec sheet on a product, or he may be taking notes on the customer's issues, problems, and things they want to do if they had the solution.

Social media doesn't change the fundamentals of the relationship between the company and the customer. It provides a channel to extend those relationships far beyond what is possible in the physical realm.

> If you put a social media lens on the sales process, you can be out listening to customers and prospects and providing value, in the solutions you provide, the information you share with your community or a contact you can offer to help them with another issue. You're no longer confined to the physical spaces. Your sales team doesn't have to hop on an airplane. You can find prospects around the world and have meaningful dialog with them.

But the bottom line, as always, is the bottom line. Building relationships isn't an end in itself. It's a proven way to build a reliable and sustainable funnel of leads. The good news is you already know what to do with a lead. Leads that come from social media may look a bit different on the front end, but on the back end, they're all the same.

> When companies first start using social media in a business-to-business context, the inclination is to say "I've started a Twitter account and I have X number of followers," or "I have been retweeted X number of times." But what you're really looking for is quality of contact, not quantity. You start measuring that by the sales funnel.

> You can use social media to drive people to your business Website. Content marketing is one way to do that: sharing white papers, case studies, blog posts, and videos. All those things point people to your Website. Include a call to action that requires the prospect to give you their contact information, and that's the first step of your lead.

The leads that came from social media can go into whatever your lead monitoring platform it is, whether it's a full-blown CRM system or something as simple as an Excel spreadsheet. That lead is real. You qualify it, and, if appropriate, you pass it on to your sales team.

It's no different from someone calling your 800 number or redeeming a coupon or coming to your booth at a trade show. If you can track those leads, you can track social media leads just as easily.

## B2B AND PHONEBOOTH-TO-B

Phonebooth.com is a North Carolina–based company that offers a cloud-based business phone system aimed at small businesses, start-ups, and entrepreneurs. The company has found that social media provides a perfect way for it to connect to its customers and prospects. Or, more accurately, to connect its customers and prospects with its corporate spokesbooth.

The company's logo and de facto mascot is a red English-style phone booth. Icons hardly get more iconic than that. Chris Moody, Phonebooth's social marketing manager, has turned the booth into a character and taken advantage of its personality (boothanality?) to build up a following on Twitter, Facebook, and Flickr.

We have a product with an image you can market to. The phone booth is iconic. We made it a character. We didn't just want to be a traditional, boring telecom company.

Twitter is the natural extension since it's a natural conversation tool. It's easy for Phonebooth to be Phonebooth. But we also rebranded our email templates, and some of our Website messaging comes from Phonebooth. When you sign up, the messages come from Phonebooth.

There's an @Phonebooth Twitter account where Phonebooth builds awareness and helps support the brand. The most important thing is to reach out to our users. Phonebooth tries to elevate users in our community. If someone talks about Phonebooth to a friend, that helps us to reach out to them, find out how they are using it and help share their stories.

The Phonebooth Twitter account is managed by Chris with support from other members of the team, who not only can log into the account but, more important, they know the tone of Phonebooth.

We're a software as a service company. The Phonebooth is sarcastic. He talks directly to people and they talk to him. We like to take the phone booth places. It catches people's attention. For some reason, people naturally want to have their picture taken with the phone booth. We shoot the pictures and ask people for their Twitter user name. We post them to our Flickr page and then reach out to them on Twitter and tell them it's there.

From there, people can use the photo however they want. We've seen people use their phone booth pictures for their Facebook and Twitter profile pictures.

We've seen a huge increase in views to our Flickr page, which helps spread the brand. When those pictures go out, they go out with "phonebooth.com" on the photo.

Chris and the Phonebooth team put in a huge push around South by Southwest (SXSW), the massive social media and Web conference in Austin, Texas, often described as "spring break for geeks." SXSW was

Phonebooth's first social media launch, and the company blew away all their numbers, for mentions, for page views, for Web conversions.

Chris took an iconic image, gave it a personality, and used social media tools to spread the word in innovative ways that customers and prospects appreciated. Some of those customers are individuals, some represent companies, and some will represent larger companies one day. Whoever your audience is, if you can capture its attention long enough to present your value proposition, you're moving in the right direction.

## TAKING AN INTEGRATED APPROACH AT CISCO

Not convinced by our example of a software-as-a-service company approaching small businesses that social media is a valuable tool for B2B? How about Cisco?

Jeanette Gibson is global director of social media at Cisco. We caught up with her and LaSandra Brill, senior manager of global social media, at a Ragan Communications social media conference held at Cisco's HQ in San Jose, California.

Cisco has fully embraced social media in a way that few large corporations have, looking across channels at all the ways it can connect with customers and prospects. It sells a wide variety of networking products and solutions to companies, small, medium, large, and enormous, but it recognizes the value and necessity of making individual connections with people.

Its social media approach incorporates blogs, Facebook, Twitter, YouTube, online communities, and social media–optimized media relations and blogger outreach as part of its PR.

Cisco's strategy also includes elements that many large companies ignore, like customizable widgets that deliver content to customers and fans, and mobile communications strategies.

The company even has a "social gaming" strategy. The myPlanNet game allows players to play the part of a CEO building his or her company from dial-up to advanced networking.

The point of all this is to extend Cisco's message in as many channels as possible and build relationships with people in the ways those people most like to interact.

Blogging is one of the pillars of the strategy. Cisco has 22 external blogs that get 475,000 views per quarter. Twenty-five percent of those blogs are video blogs, and the company has found it gets five times the level of retention of its message when it uses video, Jeanette says:

> Every person in communications and marketing at Cisco is now a publisher. If you're going to be engaging externally with our customers, we want you to shoot a video and your videos need to be "snackable," 90 seconds or less. Videos are a quick, high-impact way to convey news. We don't need to spend a month doing a press release.

Jeanette acknowledges that it's not necessarily easy to turn a global workforce into documentary filmmakers.

> Employees need to learn the basic techniques and practice. This is tough work. This is business process change. And this is why training has been so important internally, to teach employees how to integrate video.

Twitter is another important focus for the company. Cisco's CTO Padmasree Warrior, for instance, has nearly a million and a half followers (as well as an awesome name). She uses Twitter to amplify Cisco's voice, share technology insights, and get feedback on her ideas and presentations. Cisco CEO John Chambers participates in live Twitter chats where he answers questions submitted by the public Jeanette elaborates:

> For Cisco, nearly 60 percent of our conversations on the social Web are on Twitter. Two years ago that was zero. By getting your teams and executives engaged, you can shift the landscape.

> People come to Twitter first, then to the blogs, then to YouTube. Twitter is the amplification tool where people want to get information first and fast, then go to the blogs for more information.

Cisco has seen immediate benefits of this process change. Not only has embracing social media techniques allowed it to react more quickly and effectively, but also to do it for less money. Jeanette cites a savings of $250,000 for one product launch, by using blogs, video produced by employees rather than high-production-value professional video, and leveraging existing content rather than taking staff time to create new content.

LaSandra has shared a presentation on SlideShare, a site that allows you to post and search PowerPoint presentations covering nearly any business topic you can imagine. LaSandra's presentation compares side by side the numbers associated with a traditional product launch versus a social media-enabled launch.

In the traditional launch, Cisco invited the audience to San Jose. In the virtual launch, nobody had to leave their desks. Cisco calculated that alone saved the equivalent of 42,000 gallons of gas.

Around 100 people attended the physical event. The cost in airport car service alone exceeded $20,000. In the virtual launch, more than 9,000 people tuned in from 128 countries.

The traditional launch resulted in 87 articles. The virtual launch garnered 245 articles, more than 1,000 blog posts, and more than 40 million impressions.

Jeanette sees it as a shift from big, flashy product launch events to a conversation with customers and prospects that unfolds over time. That approach is proving to be both less expensive and more effective. She says:

> We saw 75 percent lower cost with increased customer
> interaction. We were able to extend our reach, have
> better conversations and spend less money.

Even so, Cisco's experiences haven't been universally positive. The more open you are and the more channels you communicate in, the more opportunities there are for people to complain and vent their spleen. "It's not always good," Jeanette says. "Let's be real." But engaging with customers who have issues gives you the opportunity not only to help resolve them but to turn negative sentiment positive.

Regardless of how you might feel about the idea of addressing customer complaints in public, that's the way it is, Jeanette says, and that's the way it will be. "This is the new expectation of how customers will interact with companies."

## WHAT YOU CAN DO RIGHT NOW

- Make a list of all the influencers in your B2B sales cycle by job type.
- Start thinking about the unique needs, wants, and interests of each group.
- Find the online communities where they congregate.
- Look at all the content you share with all those people, and find ways to share it through social media.

# CHAPTER 11

# Public Relations

*It takes 20 years to build a reputation, and five minutes to ruin it. If you think about that, you'll do things differently.*

—Warren Buffett

Both of your authors are former newspaper journalists. We love journalism and understand its vital role in our society.

Nevertheless, it's facing some big challenges. Some people say journalism as we know it is dying. Newspapers have been cutting back for years, investigative journalism is rapidly becoming a thing of the past, and few local papers have the staff to cover anything but the big stories, let alone the garden club meeting.

Niche publications in all but the largest industries are feeling the pinch as well. Maybe some of the trade publications in your industry have folded or merged with others. It's becoming harder and harder for any publication to specialize.

For years, online resources have been springing up to fill the void. Print publications are starting their own blogs. Laid-off journalists are taking their expertise and their contact lists (remember when we called it a Rolodex?) and starting blogs too, covering the same industries they used to cover in print and competing with the blogs of their previous employers.

Many of the industry journalists who are still working write for blogs as well as print, blurring the lines between blogger and journalist. And if you want to see blurry lines, try to define the differences among bloggers, journalists, analysts, and consultants. In some industries, one person might wear one, two, three, or all of those hats.

Here's the good news: With the niches your company wants to influence becoming smaller and more specialized, you can become an online influencer yourself. Yes, you.

## THE OLD MODEL OF PR

In the old model of corporate PR, the first step in getting out your message was to write a press release, using as much industry gobbledygook as possible so that people knew your industry-leading, enterprise-grade, end-to-end solution was flexible, extensible, robust, feature rich, best of breed, bleeding edge, and defined a new paradigm for your industry. The release included lots of forceful, dynamic, and confident quotes from your CEO, which he certainly didn't write and may not have even read.

You then paid to have the release put out on the wire, where no regular person was likely to find it. It got picked up by some Websites and confused all but the 3 or 5 or 15 journalists who care about your industry. They either read the first paragraph and then promptly forgot about it completely or called your company's PR team and said, "What the hell did that actually mean?"

Your corporate flack (and we use that term with love) explained the story in plain English and offered to put them in touch with the product manager. Only the laziest journalists used anything you'd written.

Or, worse, your corporate flack spent days, weeks, or months calling, emailing, calling, emailing, calling, emailing, and calling the key journalists in your industry, trying to get them to pay attention. Maybe one of the key journalists mentioned on her blog how annoying your flack was being. They'll do that sometimes.

Assuming he managed to get through, your flack arranged for the journalist to interview several key people in your company, including the CEO (who went totally off message in the interview) and the product manager (who focused on the "speeds and feeds" of the product and never actually mentioned why anybody would want to buy it). The flack then spent the next few days, weeks, or months following up with the journalist, trying to get the key messages into the piece.

You waited with bated breath for 12 hours to 12 months waiting for the story to come out, and when it did, half the facts were wrong, the quotes were out of context, and the story made a big deal out of some little feature and completely ignored the one most important thing about the product. Plus, the story included a comment from your biggest competitor saying it had been doing the same thing for a year, or an analyst who completely missed the point. Or both.

Of course, the journalists, analysts, product managers, and CEOs your authors work with on a regular basis never do things like that.

## THE NEW MODEL OF PR

In the new model of PR, you don't write a press release, hope someone sees it and writes a good story; *you* write a good story. You interview your product manager, your CEO, and your customers. You make it interesting and fun to read. You cut out the buzzwords and the gobbledygook and write like a real person talking to real people. You write a story that says "This is why this product is cool and helps people."

You post it to your blog and make sure you use all the right keywords so that search engines find it when people are looking for information about your product or your industry. Maybe you shoot a video interview with customers talking about how it solves that big problem that's been keeping them awake at night. You post that video to YouTube, tagged with all those same keywords.

You promote it on Twitter, on your company LinkedIn and Facebook groups, and in every other way you can. (More about that later.)

Then you answer the phone when a reporter calls. Like Lee Aase did.

## SOCIAL MEDIA PR AT MAYO CLINIC

Lee Aase is manager of syndication and social media at Mayo Clinic in Rochester, Minnesota, and a man with even more innovative ideas than he has vowels. Lee was an early convert to the value of social media for PR.

Lee's advice for PR professionals is as simple as it is profound: "Don't just pitch the media, be the media."

> We started our social media efforts as a way to do our public relations better. It was about me being more effective using these power tools to accomplish the work I was hired to do. Whether it's Twitter or Facebook or YouTube or blogs (the four food groups in our pyramid), they enable in-depth communications with journalists and with the general public, who are our eventual audience and the people we most want to influence.

> We use these tools to provide information to journalists on a pre-embargo basis when we have a story we're pitching, or to provide audio or video of one of our subject matter experts. But we also want to make that in-depth information available to the public and potential patients.

Lee created a "social media newsroom," using the WordPress blog platform, that met all of his team's needs. Soon the team was sharing blog posts and video interviews featuring Mayo's doctors. If a major medical story like swine flu hit the news and a Mayo doctor had expertise in that area, a member of Lee's team would rush to that doctor's office with a small, handheld video camera and a tripod, shoot a short interview with the doctor discussing what people should know about the subject, and have the video edited and posted to the social media newsroom by the end of the day.

The videos were a bit rough and didn't match the production values of the ones shot by Mayo's video team, but they were fast, timely, and relevant. Lee found that not only were the quick videos getting lots of views, they were also getting the attention of the mainstream media. The *Wall Street Journal* quoted one of the doctors Lee interviewed. CBS Radio Network took the audio from one of the clips and used it on its national broadcast.

Because Lee posted interesting interviews that gave people real information, Mayo's audience grew and its reach expanded. And he did it all without begging a journalist to call him back.

Even so, Lee fully understands and appreciates the value of a Mayo mention in a major national or regional publication. Those stories go a long way toward spreading important news and raising Mayo's profile.

Any PR practitioner knows the value of a story in *USA Today*. They also know that it can take years of pitching, relationship building, and rejection before it happens.

The Mayo team made it happen with a handheld video camera and a clip posted to YouTube.

Jayson Werth is an outfielder who was playing for the Los Angeles Dodgers in 2005 when he was hit by a pitch in spring training. What followed were months of chronic pain that doctors couldn't diagnose and even orthopedic surgery didn't fix. Jayson thought his career was over, until a family friend, also an orthopedic surgeon, suggested he visit Mayo Clinic orthopedic surgeon Richard Berger. Dr. Berger had successfully diagnosed a type of injury to the ulnotriquetral (UT) ligament that doesn't show up on an MRI.

Jayson met with Dr. Berger, who determined he had in fact suffered a tear to his UT ligament, and was able to repair the damage. Jayson signed to the Philadelphia Phillies and two years later found himself playing in the World Series.

Lee saw the potential for a great story and pitched it to the national media. For whatever reason, he couldn't get their attention. But he didn't forget about it.

> Seven months later I was in Philadelphia with my video camera. I interviewed Jayson in the dugout. When they qualified for the World Series, my colleague Amy Tieder, who is building our *USA Today* relationship, was able to use that YouTube video of Jayson and our blog posts about his surgery to pitch the story. *USA Today* picked it up and did a half-page story on the UT ligament issue and how Jayson's career was saved.

A great outcome for the Mayo Clinic indeed, but Lee didn't stop there. He saw another way to extend the reach of the story via Twitter.

Lee and Amy suggested to *USA Today* that it do a live Twitter chat, and the paper liked the idea. Dr. Berger went on Twitter and answered questions about this common but undiagnosed wrist injury.

> Five months later, I saw a blog post from a young woman in Washington, D.C. named Erin Turner. Because of this Twitter chat, she was able to get the same diagnosis, went to see Dr. Berger, and had her wrist operated on. She's 28 years old and had been in chronic pain for five years. She'd seen an orthopedic surgeon in D.C. who could only suggest fusing her wrist, although he said he wouldn't recommend it. He didn't have anything to offer. Because of the in-depth resources that allowed her to diagnose herself, she was able to get relief.

A great story got even better when Lee closed the loop. When the Phillies opened their season in Washington, D.C., Lee arranged for Erin to meet Jayson and thank him for sharing his story. *USA Today* covered their meeting.

Lee is proud of the stories that the Mayo Clinic team placed using social media tools, but he's even more proud of the good they did.

> A big part of my job for Mayo is to get national media stories. This is our ultimate case study: two national stories that would have been extremely unlikely without YouTube and Twitter. And most importantly, a patient and many others like her were able to get help because we could make this information available.

## SOCIAL MEDIA IN A CRISIS

Lee Aase showed us some ways to use social media to get the media and the public talking about you when the story is good. What do you do when the story is bad?

In the old days, if somebody said something bad about your company, it was often a good idea to wait and see what came of it. Unless you knew the person with the beef was highly influential, you had time to gauge the impact and formulate a response. Maybe you would decide to ignore him altogether.

Ask Nestlé and BP how that strategy works in a social media world. With the growth of social media, everyone is influential. Yes, some people still have a broader and deeper reach than others, but the complaints of one person or a small group can quickly gain momentum and notoriety and erupt into a global firestorm while your PR team is scheduling a response meeting.

Furthermore, as search engines like Google and social networks like Facebook place higher and higher value on the connections within a person's "social graph," one person's voice can speak louder than that of thousands. It probably wouldn't worry you too much if one person out there thought your product was bad or your customer service rude. But what if that one person is a Facebook friend of the CEO you're pitching?

## GREENPEACE VERSUS NESTLÉ

In early 2010, Nestlé faced a coordinated attack from Greenpeace over allegations that suppliers of palm oil purchased by the global conglomerate were clear-cutting rain forests and destroying animal habitats. As part of its protest, Greenpeace created an altered version of the KitKat candy bar package (KitKats are produced by Hershey in the United States but Nestlé in other parts of the world) with the logo changed to read "Killer." It also posted a video to YouTube showing a consumer unwrapping a KitKat and finding an orangutan's finger.

Within hours, Greenpeace supporters had posted the video to their Facebook pages and shared it on Twitter. Many changed their Facebook profile pictures to the altered "Killer" logo and posted to Nestlé's corporate Facebook page expressing their outrage.

Nestlé's PR response was straight out of the traditional PR playbook. It asked YouTube to take down the video, but by then it had spread beyond anyone's ability even to find the many places it had been posted. It also threatened to remove any postings from its Facebook page from commenters displaying the "Killer" logo.

This response merely fanned the flames. The Nestlé Facebook page was inundated with negative comments at such a rate and frequency that social media bloggers were debating whether the company could ever regain control of it. Some argued that Nestlé should declare defeat and pull down the page.

Months after the height of the attack, Nestlé's Facebook page had settled down and the company was sharing a great deal of information about its environmental focus, including posts about palm oil and its efforts to pressure suppliers to eliminate any sources of palm oil that are related to rain forest destruction.

Each of these posts engenders dozens of comments, some of them positive, some of them negative, some of them juvenile and off topic. Many people indicate their support of particular postings by clicking on Facebook's thumbs-up "like" icon. Even so, there appears to be little interaction on the part of Nestlé with the members of the public who visit its Facebook page.

## THE POWER OF PARODY

At the time we're writing this book, the oil well tragedy in the Gulf of Mexico is still in the news, despite the well having been declared "effectively dead." The aftermath will drag on, no doubt, for years, as will the memory of how the crisis played out in social media. BP's PR response to the spill has been generally reviled, and was summed up in a *Newsweek* piece by Alan Mascarenhas:

> The first disaster was the oil spill. The second was BP's public relations. Since the Deepwater Horizon rig sank more than a month ago, the company's response has ranged from awkward to awful, causing offense all over again with inappropriate statements and tone-deaf tweets.

We won't pile on. Whether judged by a traditional media or social media approach, this has been a PR calamity.

One of the most poignant lessons learned centers around a Twitter account. A fake Twitter account. Using the Twitter name BPGlobalPR, someone calling himself "Leroy Stick" began issuing phony tweets purporting to be from the company.

Intended to highlight what many saw as a callous response from the company (typified by then-CEO Tony Hayward's comment, "I'd like my life back"), the imposter account sent tweets like these:

> Here's the thing: we made $45 million A DAY in profits in 2009. This really isn't a big deal.

> People are upset, so we are working nonstop to make as
> many "BP cares" shirts as we can.
>
> Restaurants across the country are celebrating the 86th
> day of the spill by declaring an 86 on seafood. That's
> good right?

As of October 2010, BP's official, actual Twitter account (BP_
America) has about 18,000 followers. The fake account has more than
188,000. Why are more people following the fake account? For one
thing, the fake account was timely and started responding to the spill
on Twitter before BP itself did.

For another, many of the tweets are funny. It's no mystery that
people need relief from tragedy, and the phony account provided a
little dark humor among the relentless scenes of environmental
catastrophe.

Shel Holtz is a consultant with more than 30 years' experience in
the corporate communications trenches. He's also a blogger, podcaster,
and speaker highly regarded for his thoughts on social media in the
corporate world, especially in regard to PR and crisis communications.
Shel talked to us about what companies can learn from BP's social
media experience.

> First of all, they can learn that news and opinions spread
> much faster than ever, through status updates tools like
> Twitter and Facebook. You have issues and events that
> can spread to the audience with unprecedented speed.
> You used to have time to consider a response, but now
> things happen in a matter of minutes.
>
> Second, you have far less control of the overall message
> than ever. The BPGlobalPR Twitter account is poking
> holes in the types of messages that BP and other
> organizations used to be able to send out with impunity,
> knowing it would be filtered by the media. Instead, the
> media are following what people say on Twitter and
> other channels.
>
> If we're learning anything from BP, we know that
> transparency is a requirement. If you're saying one thing
> internally and one thing externally, it will get out. There
> has to be one voice. Anything you say in one place is
> going to be said in another.

Organizations must also understand the beast that is the 24-hour news cycle. "News is now about satisfying the insatiable curiosity of the public," Shel says. Faced with a vacuum of information from the company, news outlets will fill airtime with whatever they can. Your company needs to be one of the sources feeding into the stream, and social media is an ideal way to do that.

Shel sums up an effective approach to social media crisis communications in this list of strategies:

- Respond quickly, accurately, professionally, and with care.
- Be transparent and accessible.
- Treat perceptions as fact.
- Acknowledge mistakes.
- Tailor messages to address the "angry" party.
- Note the other side's concerns.
- Make no public confrontations.
- Emphasize existing relationships.

"Leroy Stick" himself posted on a blog called Street Giant a rationale for his actions with the BPGlobalPR Twitter account that not only sums up the threat social media can pose to unresponsive companies but the ethos behind much of social media in general:

> I know that at the end of the day BPGlobalPR is just a Twitter account. I know I'm not changing the world, but I'm doing SOMETHING. If you take anything away from BPGlobalPR, let it be that your little idea could work. The Internet offers a pretty accessible audience, so why not try and start something? We can use new media to affect the old. We can change the conversation. We can set a new standard for corporate responsibility if we just make the choice to attack corporate irresponsibility. Let's show these people that they can't get away with business as usual anymore. All I'm asking of you, the reader, is to TRY. Just TRY. You'll be surprised what can happen.

# WHAT YOU CAN DO RIGHT NOW

▪ Start thinking like a publisher. Look at all the channels you have to share information with your customers and prospects.

▪ Think about the stories you can share that would inform and excite someone who doesn't know anything about your company or your product.

▪ Make sure your PR team is aware of—and using—the tools discussed in Chapter 7.

▪ Develop a social media crisis response plan.

▪ Register all the Web URLs and Twitter user names someone might use to make your company look bad.

# CHAPTER 12

# Sales

*You will make more friends in a week by getting yourself interested in other people than you can in a year by trying to get other people interested in you.*

—Arnold Bennett

Let's not beat around the bush here: Salespeople are hard to convince when it comes to trying new tactics. They're busy, they're bottom-line driven, and they want to do what works. Come to them with something unproven and pie in the sky, and you'll find yourself talking to a rapidly vanishing backside.

But if you can convince a salesperson of the value of a new tool, you'll not only have a violent convert on your hands, you'll also soon have all of her closest colleague/competitors breaking down your door, asking for the same advantage.

Even if all of your knowledge of sales comes from the movie *Glengarry Glen Ross*, you already know what is nearest and dearest to a salesperson's heart: qualified leads. (Also, coffee is for closers.)

How much are you paying for leads? Many organizations know their cost for a qualified sales lead. Depending on the type of product, the cost of a lead can climb to hundreds of dollars. Maybe more.

Here's the good news: You can get some of the most qualified leads imaginable just by opening your social media ears and listening. According to a 2009 survey by the IT Services Marketing Association, 75 percent of corporate IT buyers use social media to gather information and communicate with colleagues during the buying process.

In other words, not only are prospective customers out there looking for information, they are telling people what they are looking for. They are venturing out into social media and asking "I'm ready to give someone a big pile of money. Who should I give it to?" Perhaps your sales teams would like to be there to help them answer that question?

Annette Green is general manager of the communications, entertainment, and media business unit at SAS. She was an early convert to the value of social media for sales. In 2008, she and members of her team were using LinkedIn and Twitter to find out more about not only the markets they serve but the people they wanted to reach. How? Because those people were freely sharing that information, Annette says, in places like LinkedIn and Twitter.

> When you're targeting an industry, it's very important to do as much research as possible. If I'm going to an event with 200 CIOs and CTOs, I might only know a handful of them. To get the most out of my time, I want to make sure I have as much background on them as possible, so that when I'm introduced to them or approach them at a booth, I can engage them on a topic that I know is going to hit the mark. I can tell them, "I saw that paper you wrote, or that presentation you made," and make a connection with them that moves the conversation forward.

> It's amazing what people are putting out there about themselves. Not only do they put information about their current employer, but they put their past work history. Sometimes I can make a connection with someone in an account that I've worked in the past. People put their slide presentations on their LinkedIn profile, connected to a SlideShare account, so you can see what topics they're interested in discussing. They'll tell you what they're reading and who influences them. Oftentimes they'll have links to a personal blog. It's a wealth of information.

It's also helpful to go behind the scenes and do some
research on who their networks are. You can view the
connections they have and find common contacts, and
that's very useful as well.

Annette and her team have found that people aren't just sharing
connection information on LinkedIn, they're also talking about the
business issues that are keeping them up at night. How valuable would
it be to your sales team to know that a prospective customer had asked
a question in a LinkedIn group to help him make a buying
decision?

Sometimes they pose a question in a group. One of the
most effective tactics I've seen is to join a professional
association on LinkedIn in your market. For example, our
vertical is media. There are a number of professional
associations out there, and executives that are part of
those will often post a discussion topic, especially if
they're doing some research and are trying to gather
information. So it's a really easy entree for you to come
in and offer helpful advice and establish a connection.

Yeah, but how do you do that without sounding stalker-y, or like
a typical salesperson? Patty Hager on Annette's team has some experience in approaching people the right way on LinkedIn.

The appropriate thing is to know the person first before
you link to them. At some industry events, when I
introduced myself to people, I would ask after we
exchanged cards, "Do you mind if I link to you?" That
provides a great forum, because you can see what other
executives they are connected to, and that can help you
get a personal introduction.

LinkedIn suggests that you not connect to people to whom you
have no connection already. And we all know that is a custom, as
Hamlet would say, more honor'd in the breach than the observance.
There are LinkedIn power users who pride themselves on the size of
their networks, and many of them build their numbers by approaching people they don't know. This tactic can have varying degrees of
success. If you're trying to connect to a CIO, and you're a sales rep
for a software company and the two of you have never met, your

reasons for requesting the connection will likely be pretty obvious. Don't be surprised if your connection request is rejected.

There is one thing many LinkedIn users agree on: If you're requesting a connection to someone you don't know or met in passing, for the love of all that is holy, personalize the message that LinkedIn sends with the introduction request. Nothing says "I'm in a hurry to get as many connections as possible" more loudly and clearly than sending the standard "I'd like to add you to my professional network" message. Your request is much more likely to be well received if you say, "We seem to share similar interests in particle acceleration," or "We met at the National Association of Underwater Taxidermists conference in Poughkeepsie. I spilled pomegranate juice on your man purse."

All of this starts with using the search functionality built into each of the major social media channels to find where people are talking about your market—or your company. LinkedIn has active groups on nearly every business topic you can imagine, and Facebook is rapidly catching up, with more and more business-related groups every day.

On Twitter, you can use the search function to find people talking about keywords and topic in your industry. If you sell oscillation overthrusters, do a Twitter search to see who is tweeting with those words. Follow that person, and see who they follow. See if they've created any Twitter lists related to their profession. That can be a quick and easy way to follow multiple people who share your professional interests.

Hashtags are another way to find relevant conversations on Twitter. Hashtags are a convention developed by Twitter users where they include a string of text after a # sign, as a way to group tweets and make them searchable. SAS, for instance, used #pbls10 on Twitter when discussing its 2010 Premier Business Leadership Series event. SAS people and attendees were encouraged to use the tag. You can use hashtag searches to find people discussing a particular event, topic, product, idea—nearly anything you can imagine.

And again, consider the value in being there "before the ask." Effective sales relationships have always been built on trust and personal contact. If your sales teams can figure out ways to be genuinely helpful in LinkedIn groups, on blogs, on Twitter, and in communities related to your business, that will make it much more likely that potential customers will seek them out when they're ready to buy what you're selling.

So if you're a salesperson, or a person who loves a salesperson, you're probably asking yourself "How am I supposed to add all this to my plate if I'm always being closing? How much time does all this take?" Patty has an answer.

> I would say I'm probably spending about two hours per week, and a lot of that is downtime, like when I'm traveling. You can quickly reference your social media channels on your mobile device. I'm also doing it any time I have a conversation with a new executive, to better get to know them.

Keep in mind that prospecting and connecting with people is a large part of Patty's job, so two hours a week might even be on the high end. Others have told us that they set aside 15 minutes a day for social media prospecting during the workweek. It all depends on your goals, and how much value you get once you start experimenting with social media as a lead generation tool. You may find that you're spending less time on less valuable activities and more on social media as it proves its worth.

If you're still on the fence, Annette says the time is now.

> Just dive in and get started. If you're in sales and you're focused on a specific vertical, it's a good idea to beef up the information in your resume about that vertical, so that when people are looking on LinkedIn for expertise, they find you, which is just as important as finding them.

Take your contact list and search for the connections you already have in your database. Pick an account or two and do some searches on that prospect or customer and see what you find. Get comfortable with how to use the tool and get started with simple, low-risk activities like information gathering and research.

Referrals and recommendations within LinkedIn are also a powerful tool for making connections, Annette says. People will obviously be more likely to trust you if you come recommended by others or, even better, by mutual connections.

If you have customers or partners you've worked with whom you know would give you an excellent recommendation, you can show that on your profile and build up your personal brand. I've had customers say very nice things about me on my LinkedIn profile, and that's helped me differentiate myself as a value partner.

What could be better than having an existing customer say nice things about you on your LinkedIn profile that potential customers will see when you link to them?

## TURNING TWITTER CONNECTIONS INTO SALES LEADS

Twitter is a great way to create and extend personal relationships, but some salespeople are still having a hard time seeing how it can apply to business relationships. Allison Green and Craig Duncan of SAS learned the value in 28 minutes.

In early 2010, Allison was following tweets from *Sports Business Journal*'s World Congress of Sports event. SAS at the time had just launched its sports analytics business, and Allison, a big sports fan herself, was keeping an eye on the event via Twitter.

At 10:39 a.m., Allison sent a tweet that read "Wishing I was at the World Congress of Sports in LA #sbjwcs." (#sbjwcs is the hashtag created for the event, to allow Twitter users to follow all the tweets on that subject.)

Ten minutes later, she noticed she'd picked up a new follower, and looked him up on LinkedIn. He turned out to be an influential sports blogger. A few minutes later she got another follower, who turned out to be a senior sports marketing executive for an NFL team.

Allison emailed her colleague Craig Duncan, who was at the event, and told him about her new follower. Turns out Craig had made inroads with the team and was trying to lock down an onsite meeting. Allison's new contact was exactly the person he needed to meet.

Allison and her new contact tweeted back and forth. She shared some information about SAS sports analytics offerings, and he was very interested. (He even retweeted one of Allison's tweets that mentioned SAS' sports analytics solution, forwarding it to all of his nearly 1,700 followers.) Allison pointed the exec to Craig's Twitter account, where he was posting notes from the conference. The executive connected with Craig, and Craig got his meeting.

There's no convert like a violent convert. Craig was sold on the value of Twitter.

> I was skeptical about Twitter but this made me a big believer. Not only did we get a meeting with a senior vice president of a major sports franchise, but he's helping us spread the message about our SAS for Sports offerings with his followers. Absolutely incredible.

## A DEBT OF GRATITUDE

One of the key lessons we hope you're getting from this book is that social media cannot be contained in the existing corporate silos we've come to know. We've agreed that customer service is the new PR. We've agreed that, in Joseph Jaffe's words, retention is the new acquisition. We've heard people tell us that social media needs to be integrated across the enterprise for it to be effective.

Here's a case study that blurs the lines among sales, marketing, and customer service and reinforces the message we heard from Zena Weist at H&R Block: If you give people good content and show them you understand their needs, they will come back to you when they're ready to buy. Social media can not only generate leads but can convert those leads into sales.

Nichole Kelly is social media director for CareOne Services, Inc. We first met her in Chapter 7. One of CareOne's social media initiatives is an online community that has been active for more than six years, with blogs, forums, and groups. Just like H&R Block, CareOne makes the community open to anyone who wants to join. As a result, it has more than 1 million members. The goal, Nichole says, is to turn more of those members into customers. The challenge is to show potential customers they can trust CareOne.

> In our industry, there are lots of trust issues. People want to see if you're a legitimate company that's not going to take advantage of them.

The key is a carefully considered content strategy aimed at providing real value to people considering debt relief. CareOne supports two major forums, "Ask the Community," where members help answer one another's questions, and "Ask the CareOne Expert," where certified debt counselors weigh in with answers.

> We post anywhere from 3 to 5 posts a day, up to about 20 a week. The forums are the most active place in the community. We've seen a lot of prospective customers asking questions in the Ask the CareOne Expert forum to see if we're a good fit for them.

CareOne connects the community to its internal customer relationship management database, so it knows which members are current customers and which are solid leads.

> We're averaging about 75,000 unique visitors a month; 15,000 log in and 6,000 of those are verified prospects. They're looking and exploring. We've also found that the people who sign up for a plan that interacted with the community convert far better. There are two major points in our sales process after someone fills out a lead form: when they sign a contract for our services and when they make their first payment. Our community has drastically improved the propensity for new leads to finish the sales process. We saw over a 200 percent improvement in leads that signed a contract over traditional channels and over a 700 percent improvement in making their first payment over traditional channels. Since making a payment is when we show revenue, that's a number that makes people take notice.

One of the ways CareOne ensures the success of its community, Nichole points out, is by providing valuable, interesting content to visitors.

> We need to provide them a different kind of content that isn't just "buy now" but gives them information they need to make their decision. We've written blog posts like "Questions You Should Ask Before Signing Up for a Debt Relief Plan." We give them the questions to vet our competitors against us. If we provide the content that will let you compare, you'll come back to the people who gave you the information in the first place.

It's one thing to make contact with people who are in dire need of debt relief. What if you can connect with them earlier, and establish a relationship before things get drastic?

> Our company typically connects with people who need an emergency room. They convert very quickly. We want to use social media to connect with them earlier, before they even know they might need us.

CareOne created a series for YouTube called "Financially Fit TV," designed to help people better manage their finances. Hosted by Nichole herself, the videos also include appearances by CareOne's "Debt Diva," Clarky Davis, with "her tips to be frugally fabulous."

From the very first episode, Financially Fit TV has shown its value as a tool to drive traffic to the CareOne Website. In a world where positive click-through results are often expressed in single digits, CareOne has seen significantly more impressive numbers.

> Half the people who watched the video came to our site, even though there was no clear hyperlink to click on. Half the people who watched the video searched us out and came to our site.

Approaching the sensitive subject of debt relief in a straightforward and honest manner has helped CareOne establish relationships with the community of bloggers who write about debt relief, whom Nichole describes as "tough nuts to crack." Not only have CareOne's social media efforts won the attention and respect of the bloggers, but Financially Fit TV has turned CareOne into an influential media outlet in its very own marketplace.

> Financially Fit TV has allowed us to have daily conversations with bloggers about the services we provide and how we help people. Instead of needing to reach out to the top bloggers, they're now approaching us. We created our very own media outlet for a small amount of money, and now we're a media outlet for them as well.

## WHAT YOU CAN DO RIGHT NOW

- Get your sales teams on Twitter and LinkedIn and encourage them to connect with your existing customers and prospects. It won't take them long to figure out the value of doing so.

- Search for industry keywords in all the major social media channels, and start building a list of the people and groups who influence your customers.

- Practice what Christopher S. Penn of Blue Sky Factory (mentioned in Chapter 7) calls "listening for intent." Set up Twitter searches and Google Alerts for keywords related to your product or industry vertical, and include words like "recommend" and "suggest" as part of the search. With any luck, you'll find prospects asking questions that could lead to valuable market intelligence or an actual lead.

# CHAPTER 13

# The Voice of the Customer

*Customer service isn't a chore. It's the new PR.*

—Chris Brogan

## CUSTOMER SERVICE

We hope by now you've accepted the idea that social media connects people and spreads messages—both good and bad—with lightning speed. If someone says something good about your company on the Web (or something bad), it has the potential to be seen instantly by tens or hundreds or thousands or hundreds of thousands of people. You know that; it's why you're still reading.

Imagine you're heading out on a Saturday to buy a new mobile phone. You walk into the big electronics store and a dozen things hit you at once: Music is playing, people are wandering about, tables and shelves are covered with merchandise. You walk through the store and see that your favorite band from college has a new CD. Televisions, you are astonished to notice, have grown another 25 percent larger than the last time you looked. Someone is trying out car stereos, and the thumping bass rattles your fillings.

You come to the mobile phone section. The clerk says, "May I help you?"

"Yes," you reply. "I'm here to buy the new Hamanaramana Millennial × 12i."

The clerk rolls his eyes, heaves a contemptuous sigh and says, "Do you live under a rock? We've been sold out for a week."

Of all the things you experienced from the time you walked into the store, which one are you most likely to remember and tell people about?

Customer service is the new PR, and we're not the first people to say it, by any means. (Chris Brogan said it sometime in 2008, and Steve Rubel used it as the title of a blog post in March 2009.) In the age of social media, the good work of your communications department over the course of months or years can be undone by one bad customer experience if it gets retold often enough.

Smart companies are integrating social media into their customer service to make sure they're doing real-time reputation management at the same speed that word travels via the Web.

## COMCAST CARES

One of the best examples comes from Comcast and its ComcastCares Twitter account. The story has been told before, so if it's old hat to you, feel free to skip ahead a bit. In short, a Comcast customer service manager named Frank Eliason took it on himself to use Twitter to help respond to customer questions and complaints.

When he started in early 2008, Comcast had some problems to deal with, including negative comments on blogs, on Twitter, and in other social media channels. Someone had even posted a video to YouTube of a Comcast cable repair person who fell asleep on a customer's couch while he was on hold with the office. (The video has had more than 1.5 million views.)

Frank decided to interact with customers in those channels, primarily reaching out and offering to help. Customers were surprised and delighted to find they weren't just tweeting into the void. Frank found how quickly a vocal, angry customer could be turned around with a little personal attention. Most people, as we all know, just want to know they're being heard.

Two years later, Frank has moved on to become senior vice president of social media at Citi, having built a team that continues to help Comcast's customer satisfaction numbers to climb. The work that Frank and his team have done in improving Comcast's image with its existing customers speaks far more loudly than any press release possibly could.

## NOTHING IS CERTAIN BUT TWITTER AND TAXES

Not only is customer service the new PR, but customer retention is the new acquisition, according to Joseph Jaffe in his book *Flip the Funnel*. And few things are as effective in retaining a customer as providing excellent customer service.

We've all heard how much more difficult and expensive it is to acquire a new customer than it is to keep an existing one. H&R Block has pioneered a groundbreaking, comprehensive social media approach to customer retention that is built squarely around providing help and assistance. The company created it with full confidence that the bottom-line benefits of retention will follow, and it has the numbers to support that confidence.

H&R Block launched an initiative called Get It Right with the express purpose of answering people's tax questions. Its business goal in creating the community was customer retention. (And, brilliantly, H&R Block's advisors will answer anyone's questions. They don't ask if you're an H&R Block customer.)

H&R Block faces competition from a variety of different areas: from mom-and-pop tax preparers, to tax software like Turbotax, to the practice of doing your own taxes. The company has a number of assets to call on, including many offices across the United States (95 percent of Americans are within five miles of an office, Zena says), a strong brand, a broad customer base, and a network of 100,000 trained tax professionals.

Why not use that network to help customers at the time they need it most? What better way to remind people of the value of an experienced tax professional than to provide a place for customers to ask questions of those professionals, quite possibly in the middle of a sleepless night, with visions of tax jail dancing in their heads?

Zena explained the thinking behind the community, which in some ways runs counter to the practice of building a large community and letting the users help one another.

> With taxes, our clients and prospects don't want their peers to answer their questions. They want experts. We're taking that community model and taking a more one-to-one route. We're kind of going retro, but it works for the expertise we bring to the table.

> We came up with the community idea on our own site to promote the expertise of our 100,000 tax professionals. When people think of H&R Block, they think of tax expertise. It's our people who represent that expertise.

The company identified 1,000 of its tax pros, gave them an introduction to the Get It Right community, and educated them on how they could and should interact with customers. The model was simple, Zena says.

> Any question that came in, we answered it for free. If we attracted more customers, that was great, but we focused on retention. It was about servicing our clients and being there with our expertise to help them through the process.

The original target had been to answer customer questions within 24 hours. Once the community was up and running, they got the average down to three hours. Zena points out the obvious value of keeping that number low. When people are doing their taxes, they want answers quickly.

When looking at the success of the Get It Right initiative, the numbers are as easy to comprehend as they are impressive. During the 2010 tax season, 135,000 customers who had visited the Get It Right community went on within the next 30 days either to purchase the company's digital tax software or to file their taxes through the H&R Block online service.

Admirable and measurable, yes, but Zena's team was measured not on the number of customers retained but on the number of questions answered and numbers of active participants. H&R Block exceeded its targets for both measures.

The focus on participation, Zena says, is a reflection of the fact that H&R Block's senior leadership fully understands and values the concept of serving the community and keeping customer service as the key goal. They know the bottom-line benefit will follow.

Zena sums up her team's philosophy of customer service in social media: listening, engaging, and responding.

> It's listening to what your clients want and making sure your strategy aligns with what your customers are saying out there. If you can respond to them, with retention comes acquisition.

> We're trying to listen to what our clients and prospects want. We don't wedge ourselves into the conversation. If they ask, we respond with one brand voice. We practice active listening, by responding to the request without pushing out a marketing message. That's a tough formula. For us it's about being a part of the conversation where it's appropriate and providing needed content.

Because of the cyclical nature of tax preparers' work, Zena also tries to think about what they can do in the off season. The trick there, she says, is to be there before the "ask." In other words, use your knowledge and expertise to provide your customers and prospects with information they need before they know they need it.

> We're on 24/7 during tax season, then we go into this quiet mode where people don't want to talk about taxes. In that period, we're there before the ask. We're providing information to help them get ready.

During the off season, H&R Block may use the community to offer tips on getting the best refund you can and how to stay prepared for filing. If you're donating to charity, for instance, don't forget to ask for receipts. That's the kind of suggestion that won't be helpful if you hear it at 11:59 p.m. on April 15.

One of the most important things to consider, according to Zena, is the totality of the message you are sending to your customers and the value they derive from you. If you're giving them what they need year round, they'll be there when it's time to make the purchase.

You have to give before you take. You can't just go dark preseason and postseason then start shoving tax messages down their throat.

## PRODUCT DEVELOPMENT

We've talked a lot about the fact that your customers are out there in social media talking about your industry, your competitors, your company, and your products. If you can use that information to craft a better marketing message, how about using it to create a better product?

Once again, the data that cost you lots of money to glean from focus groups and market research is being freely offered up in social media, if you take the time (and install the tools) to hear it.

One of the best-known examples of product development using social collaboration tools is Dell's IdeaStorm, launched in 2007 "as a way to talk directly to our customers." Here's some background from the IdeaStorm website:

> IdeaStorm was created to give a direct voice to our customers and an avenue to have online "brainstorm" sessions to allow you the customer to share ideas and collaborate with one another and Dell. Our goal through IdeaStorm is to hear what new products or services you'd like to see Dell develop. We hope this site fosters a candid and robust conversation about your ideas.
>
> In almost three years, IdeaStorm has crossed the 10,000 idea mark and implemented nearly 400 ideas! As Dell is always moving forward and innovating, so is IdeaStorm. In addition to the open discussion IdeaStorm site, in December 2009, Dell added "Storm Sessions" where Dell posts a specific topic and asks customers to submit ideas.

In other words, Dell has gotten 400 ideas that helped it improve existing products or develop new products. Products it can sell. Dell has found the whole thing to be so successful that now the company is not just soliciting random ideas, it's creating virtual focus groups. Customers are refining Dell's product ideas before the products go into production, ensuring that what hits the market is what people want to buy.

Is anybody bringing you great new ideas for products you can sell that have already been vetted? Maybe you just need to go out and ask.

So, you're thinking, of course Dell customers are going to log in to a forum and talk about what they want. They're computer geeks. Computer geeks like to talk about computers. How will this work for me?

What if we told you there were sink mat geeks? Food storage geeks? Rubbermaid found them. Or, more precisely, the geeks found Rubbermaid, and helped the company avoid what could have been a couple of costly mistakes.

How did it start? Rubbermaid took the leap of faith and added consumer-generated product reviews to its website, allowing anyone to come to their home on the Web and say whatever they wanted about Rubbermaid products. The results were a little frightening at first, according to Bert Dumars.

When Rubbermaid launched its Produce Saver line of containers, they found that some of the reviewers hated them and some loved them. The ones that hated them said their fruits and vegetables were actually spoiling faster—the exact opposite of the intended outcome.

> Because people feel these products are very simple, they throw the instructions away without reading them. The instructions in this case said you shouldn't wash or cut vegetables before putting them into the containers.

Based on the initial reviews, Rubbermaid made the instructions more prominent and went from 72 percent negative reviews to 92 percent positive. And positive reviews help to sell products. "Consumers trust each other more than they trust a company," Bert says.

Rubbermaid had a similar experience when it changed the way it made sink mats. Engineers had determined that adding an antibacterial agent to the mats would be a positive change that consumers would appreciate. Consumers did, until they noticed—and complained vociferously online—that the mats were staining. Turns out that in order to add the antibacterial agent, Rubbermaid had removed the antistaining agent.

> We started getting bad reviews, including one from someone who'd been buying our sink mats for 40 years.

> People told us, "I buy these things to make my sink
> look better. I'll pour bleach on it myself to kill the
> bacteria."

> Our research showed that antibacterial would be good. It
> didn't find that reducing anti-stain properties would
> negate the benefit of the antibacterial improvement in
> consumers' eyes.

Rubbermaid listened and made the change, and rolled it out to its new online focus group.

> The people who complained the loudest got the first of
> the new product. They were thrilled. They were amazed
> that Rubbermaid showed they listened and cared.

The consumers were happy to be heard, and Rubbermaid was happy for the feedback.

> This is not a high-cost item, but it's an important business
> for us, and we don't want it to die because of a mistake
> like that.

## THE PHONE IS RINGING

One of the reasons Chris Brogan gets quoted a lot in a social media context is because he says really smart, quotable things. Lots of people have proclaimed social media to be "the new something-or-other." Chris calls it the new dial tone. It's as essential to corporate communications now and in the future as telephone service was in the twentieth century.

So it's fitting we should include an example of how Phonebooth.com used the new dial tone to make a better phone service for its customers.

Chris Moody of Phonebooth.com describes the system it uses to gather feedback, built around the company's forum at feedback.bandwidth.com, which is powered by the UserVoice customer feedback tool.

> It gives users the ability to go in and request features and
> say what they like and don't like. We also get a lot of
> feedback by monitoring mentions on Twitter. People will

say, "This is really cool but I wish it would do this." We
can talk to them and get real feedback. It's not an
isolated data point.

Phonebooth's product development and marketing teams, including senior personnel, all read the comments and respond directly to
customers. And when they take a suggestion, they follow up and say
thanks.

When we add a feature to a product, we like to reach
back out to the people who requested it in social media
and say, "Thanks to your feedback, we've added that
feature."

Chris gives one specific example where product feedback helped
the company identify a problem that wasn't actually a problem. As
they say in software development, "It's not a bug, it's a feature."

A lot of people who were using our Phonebooth
OnDemand service talked about a delay when they
answered the phone. We were able to identify that it
wasn't a delay, it was actually a result of it being a
high-quality connection. People are used to hearing
static, but they were hearing silence. Without the social
media feedback we might not have known people were
experiencing that as a negative.

That feedback led to a blog post called "High Quality Phone
Experience and The Sound of Silence," where Chris explained the
issue. "We haven't had a complaint about an initial 'delay' since we
published that," he says.

Phonebooth found it was having a lot of people drop off somewhere in the middle of the setup process. The feedback forums told
Phonebooth that it needed a simpler process. The company responded
by creating a tool called "The Stepper," which walks new users through
the process of setting up their new phone system. It also helps to
explain any terminology that might be unfamiliar, like "auto atten-
dant" or "call groups."

As a result of The Stepper, we have fewer setup problems
for people who use it, and it gives us a better ability to
demo and walk through the set up process.

The feedback also inspired us to create a webinar called "How to Set Up Your Phonebooth Free in 15 Minutes or Less." We send it out to all customers of our free service, in case they want to come back and refresh their knowledge. The first time we presented the webinar, we had several hundred attendees. We also sent it to people who had abandoned the setup process. We recorded the webinar and put it on the Vimeo video sharing service so that we have something that sticks around.

Using social media tools not only gave Phonebooth a way to gather its customers' concerns but a channel to address them and an ongoing strategy to engage with them.

## WHAT YOU CAN DO RIGHT NOW

- Make sure your customer service and support teams are aware of—and using—the tools discussed in Chapter 7.
- Find the online communities where people are talking about your company and your products.
- Make it a part of someone's job to reach out and connect with those people, listen to their comments, and solve their problems.
- Give customers a place to tell you how to make your products better.

CHAPTER **14**

# Internal
# Communications

*The single biggest problem in communication
is the illusion that it has taken place.*

—George Bernard Shaw

Most of the enterprise social media examples that get attention involve external communications and marketing. We hope you haven't forgotten that one of your most important constituent groups is made up of your own employees. If we acknowledge the value of using social media tools to communicate with people outside the firewall, why not inside?

Studies from people like The Aberdeen Group and McKinsey have shown that companies that adopt social networking and collaboration tools perform better than those that don't.

In addition to espousing the value of social media for PR, communications consultant Shel Holtz sees the benefits internally as well. "It's incredibly valuable inside the organization," he says.

For example, social collaboration tools can be used by employees to create their own communities of practice internally, sharing information and best practices and eliminating duplication of effort. That's the kind of thing, Shel says, that companies used to pay outside consultants to figure out for them.

Messaging tools like Twitter or Yammer (a Twitter-like microblogging platform that has often been called "Twitter for the enterprise") provide a quick and easy way for employees to ask questions of one another.

> The ability to say "I'm looking for somebody inside the organization who has this particular ability" is extremely valuable. We used to just pick up the phone and say "Do you know somebody who knows something about X?" It could take days. Floating that question on an internal Twitter-like system can surface the answer in minutes.

Shel cites another example where using social networking tools helped a company get an important message heard by employees who had a long history of ignoring it.

> At BestBuy they had been trying for years to get the folks who work on the retail floor to invest in the 401k plan, but if you're a 23-year-old associate, it's a tough sell. They went out to the company's internal social network and said, "If you invest in the 401k plan, produce a video or write a blog post and tell your colleagues why you invest." They got a 40 percent increase in 401k investment from the retail workers as a result.

Internal social collaboration can have significant benefits when it comes to problem solving as well. Think back to the last really good brainstorming session you had with your team, where the collective power of your imaginations helped clarify an issue and create a solution. Internal social networking tools can help make that happen across the enterprise every day. Shel points to an example at IBM.

> At IBM, any employee can start an internal blog, and they found people were having writer's block. They started a program called the Bloggers' Muse, where employees could ask for blog posts on a topic and others could "like" that suggestion.

Not only did it help the bloggers do whatever the digital equivalent is of putting pen to paper, it showed what topics people were interested in and needed help with, and who had expertise in those topics. Employees with expertise would see that other people were looking for their knowledge.

## THE "VIRTUAL WATER COOLER"

All well and good, but before you can have meaningful interactions internally, you have to get your people to participate effectively. Len Devanna, director of digital strategy at EMC, figured out a way to make that happen. He calls it the "virtual water cooler" and describes it as one of EMC's most successful strategies.

EMC created an internal community designed not to talk about business topics but for employees to talk about whatever they wanted to discuss. More often than you might realize, employees will say they are afraid to participate in social media because they might do something wrong. Having an internal, closed network creates a feeling of comfort and helps employees get over the first hump: the first blog post, the first tweet, or the first status update.

Not only has the internal network helped employees dip a toe in the social media waters, it has also helped spur interaction and creativity. Len has seen that nonbusiness discussions can often generate ideas that turn into valuable business ideas.

The water cooler helped crowdsource ideas to improve the company's internal cell phone policy, Len says, and also generated ideas from employees on how to save the company money.

Most important, it helps employees to learn, Len says, and that learning is crucial. "These are critical skills," he says. "They will be expected in your next role, or by your next employer."

EMC has internal and external social media presences. EMC One is an internal collaboration platform that Len describes as the "seed" of everything. It has 16,000 active users and 10,000 casual users out of 44,000 employees.

EMC One incorporates employee profiles that allow it to be used as an "expertise locator" to find EMC employees with the skills needed for a project. It also creates internal affinity, Len says, and makes employees feel more connected to one another and the brand, increasing morale, productivity, and retention.

> It's now how we work. We design products, we discuss strategy, we discuss competitors. In the fall of last year it crashed for six hours and we stopped working inside. It was more impactful than email.

On that day, Len says, the company realized EMC One was a business-critical platform.

Len's advice for companies looking to incorporate social networking tools for internal collaboration is to create policies and guidelines, but then it's time to go with the flow.

> Forcing behaviors won't work. No one likes to be told what to do. Command and control is so 1.0. The key is to educate, enable, and scale. Give employees best practices to follow and playbooks that show people what a social platform is and how to use it for your business.

## SOCIAL MEDIA AND INTERNAL COMMUNICATIONS AT SAS

In 2010, *Fortune* magazine named SAS "the best company to work for in America." Two-thirds of the award is based on an anonymous survey of employees. So you know the company not only treats employees well but is committed to continuously improving the ways in which it communicates with them.

Becky Graebe is a senior manager of internal communications at SAS and a member of the company's Marketing 2.0 Council. She's been a leader in bringing social media principles to internal communications.

> It just doesn't make sense to expect employees who rely on social media in their personal lives to drop those collaboration tools when they walk in the door. The value they gain from external social media channels can also be experienced inside the company, and that includes asking questions of coworkers and management, sharing ideas and resources and providing constructive feedback.

SAS has had an active intranet for years, called the SAS Wide Web (SWW). Social features have been showing up there on a regular basis. There are more than 600 employee blogs on the SWW. Employees can set up their own bookmarks on the internal homepage and set up RSS feeds to the resources they find most useful (all a part of a major effort to prevent email overload).

Stories on the SWW, about everything from sales successes, to new product introductions, to town hall meetings led by CEO Jim Goodnight, have comments enabled so that employees can ask questions. (One of the most successful implementations of that feature came when the company crowdsourced its breakroom snack selection. Mixed nuts lost out to trail mix, in case you're wondering.)

The company also created its own internal microblogging site called Chatter. It functions essentially the same as Twitter but allows employees to keep their comments inside the firewall, giving them some measure of comfort that their updates are being shared only with colleagues.

SAS is also committed to creating an internal social network that will mirror some of the fun and functionality of Facebook while at the same time meeting a real business need to increase collaboration and communication.

Becky has several pieces of advice for internal communicators. First, make sure you have established policies and guidelines.

> Time and energy invested up front equals a multitude of time and energy saved later. Without clear guidelines, the employees you want to engage in 2.0 activities won't feel comfortable enough to do so. Those who don't bring out the best in your company will have free reign.

She also advises companies to know where to be firm and where to allow flexibility. Enforce the policies, but let employees express their individual personality and style. The online corporate directory provides a good example. For years, the directory showed employees' badge pictures. (And we all know how flattering those can be.) The only option you had was whether to display your photo on your profile page or not.

In 2009, SAS's internal communications team had the idea to let employees post whatever picture they wanted. Many used their official corporate photo, but others posted pictures taken outside of work that showed more about who they are than what you get from a stiff smile and a mottled blue background. The result was a significant increase in the number of employees who posted their pictures.

How else do you get your employees to engage? Becky offers three ways:

1. Provide them with space and purpose to get comfortable with the tools and techniques, like leaving comments, posting to microblog sites, and using custom RSS feeds.

2. Give them something to talk about.

3. Trust them and have some fun.

## WHAT YOU CAN DO RIGHT NOW

- Create safe places inside the firewall where people can experiment with social media: an internal social network, microblog (Twitter) application, internal blogs, and an internal video portal. They don't have to be fancy. A simple forum or message board can get you started.

- Build an internal social network as a way for employees to share information and expertise with one another.

- Check out Yammer, a.k.a. "Twitter for the enterprise," a microblog application that restricts access only to people on your email domain, giving some measure of privacy.

- Try a members-only LinkedIn or Facebook group as another way to let your employees try out the tools with their colleagues before venturing out into the real world.

# Intuit Social Communications Policy*

T his appendix is a "best practice" example of a written policy courtesy of Intuit.

## BACKGROUND AND PURPOSE

At Intuit, we're passionate about listening to and learning from our customers. We've been doing that for years. Today, those conversations are increasingly happening online through social media and social networks, like Facebook, blogs and Twitter—even our own Live Community. Participating in and igniting conversations is part of our overall customer experience and significantly influences how consumers think and talk about our products and brands.

These conversations are very important, so we've created some simple guidelines to help you communicate clearly in social media conversations with our customers and others who we may encourage

---

*© Intuit, Inc.

to talk openly and honestly on our behalf. This Social Communication Policy applies in our Intuit-sponsored social media/communities and in independent sites that aren't affiliated with us. Our affiliates, partners, and pro advisors can also use this Social Communication Policy to guide their conversations about Intuit and Intuit offerings.

Every Intuit employee may participate in social media conversations. It's a great way to talk about what excites you at work and, at the same time, to learn more about our customers.

Also, if you are an hourly employee, you should only participate in social media conversations about Intuit during your regular working hours.

## INTUIT'S SOCIAL COMMUNICATION GUIDING PRINCIPLES

These guiding principles support all our social media interactions. They will help you have meaningful conversations with customers while staying true to yourself and Intuit's values.

As you'll see, they'll also help us remain true to our brand attributes. In all of our social interactions about Intuit, we want to be:

- Real
- Honest
- Committed
- Smart
- Spirited

### Guiding Principle: Real

**Policy:**

- Reveal your true, authentic personality.
- Use your natural voice—no "corporate speak."
- Identify yourself as an employee of Intuit.
- Don't shout.

Social media can help you informally express yourself and your ideas. Most people who use social media appreciate the fact that they can be themselves in their communications, and they expect the same authenticity from others.

When you participate in social media or social community conversations, be yourself. When you're talking about the company and our offerings, always remember to identify yourself as an Intuit employee. Speak naturally and from the heart. Avoid corporate speak—expressing yourself authentically is the best thing you can do.

The way you express your thoughts can be as important as the thoughts themselves, so in addition to carefully reviewing the language you use, be careful to avoid the impression that you're shouting your message. In written social communication, you give the impression of "shouting" when you use all-caps in words or phrases or excessively use exclamation points or other indicators of emphasis, like bold text.

This means that you should **avoid**:

- Typing in ALL CAPS.
- Bolding or underlining words.
- Using excessive exclamation points.

You can find additional help in ensuring that your real and respectful comments will be interpreted correctly by referring to the Intuit's Code of Conduct & Ethics. Remember that Intuit's Code of Conduct & Ethics and all its related policies apply in all contexts related to Intuit, including the Internet.

Good Example: Hi folks. I work for Intuit in customer support and saw this posting—had to speak up . . .

Bad Example: To whom it may concern: The following is a response to the below posting . . .

Good Example: Thank you for your frankness in explaining your perspective. I appreciate the time you've obviously taken to explain your opinion . . .

Bad Example: WRONG!!! I can't believe that you'd say something like that.

## Guiding Principle: Honest

### Policy:

- Provide accurate and fact-based responses.
- Admit when you don't know something.
- Make it clear that your opinions are your opinions.
- Disclose any incentives or affiliations influencing your conversations.

No one expects you to know everything, and our customers will respect you for being clear about what part of your communication is fact, what part represents your opinion, and when you don't know something. A safe rule of thumb regarding facts versus opinions—if you can find a reliable source to back up your statement, do so. You should have substantiation (proof or evidence) when talking about quantifiable results you've experienced or about product performance Otherwise, it may be your opinion and you should say so. Also, remember that your opinion is your opinion—make it clear when you are expressing your opinion that it represents your personal opinion and not Intuit's.

It is also important to disclose any incentives or affiliations behind social media postings. Sometimes we (or agencies we hire) encourage people to use or talk about Intuit or our offerings through prize contests, giving away free products or other form of reward or payment. We may even work with bloggers to talk about us, and in these cases it is our responsibility to make sure the blogger also discloses his or her relationship with Intuit. Other times, we ourselves may be partially motivated by some kind of incentive. If there are incentives involved, we should always disclose them clearly.

It's important to be aware that Intuit, 3rd-party advertising networks we use, and bloggers can be held responsible for unsubstantiated or misleading advertising claims or endorsements. So, if you run a program where you are asking people to write about Intuit's offerings in exchange for something of value, remember to put in place reasonable steps to monitor those activities to ensure they are complying with our policy—and take steps to try to fix issues when they are discovered.

Good Example: Though I'm an Intuit employee, my comment here is my opinion and not Intuit's . . .

Bad Example: Here's what we at Intuit think . . .

Good Example: I did a little research on your question about what P3P means. I visited the W3C's Web site at http://www.w3.org/—if you're familiar with the W3C, you'll know that the organization is responsible for the creation of the P3P standard. Anyhow, here's the definition that the W3C provides . . .

Bad Example: Everybody knows that the definition of P3P is . . .

## Guiding Principle: Committed

### Policy:

- Listen more than you talk.
- Strive for understanding.
- Respond thoughtfully.
- Don't disparage others.
- Embrace diverse perspectives.

The most valuable part of any conversation is the information you hear and understand; not necessarily the information you impart to others. Social conversations are no exception.

Be committed to really listening and understanding. Express your interest in the opinions of others and listen—really listen—to those opinions. If you keep in mind that any social media conversation is that—a two-way conversation—and that any feedback is valuable and deserves a thoughtful response, you'll be much more likely to have a natural and productive conversation.

The great thing about any conversation is that it is a venue for people to talk about what they really care about and what's important to them. Those varied perspectives create the richness and depth of all online conversations. People participating in a social conversation may be saying negative things about Intuit. In these instances, it can be easy to fall into the trap of jumping into the conversation in Intuit's defense. Instead, really "listen" to the person's comments. This means that it's more important to focus on understanding and trying to address the concern rather than justifying Intuit's actions.

In other cases, though, you may agree with a negative reaction to an Intuit offering or action. While you can and should express your opinions truthfully, your responses should reflect an underlying assumption of Intuit's good intent.

Reviews and ratings allow customers to express their true likes and dislikes. Though rating and review systems may sometimes seem unfair or skewed, part of letting the real conversation happen is to avoid interfering with or trying to artificially influence those systems.

We must be committed to respect the opinions of others, whether or not we agree with those opinions, and make sure that our responses communicate that respect.

> Good Example: I'm committed to learning and hearing more about your thoughts. Can you help me understand more about the experience you had? . . .

> Bad Example: I don't know anything about the experience you had, but I can tell you right now that . . .

## Guiding Principle: Smart

**Policy:**

- Speak as if your words will make the front page news.
- Don't pre-announce Intuit features, offerings, or activities before they are public knowledge.
- Don't disclose Intuit confidential or personal information.
- Ask for help when in doubt.

Carefully consider your social communication BEFORE posting. It's the best way to protect yourself and Intuit against future embarrassment and even possible legal troubles. Remember that social communications can be easily misinterpreted and frequently taken out of context. A good test to use is to consider how you would feel if your communication appeared in the *Wall Street Journal*. What about in a TechCrunch article, where others may interpret and comment on what you've said? Would you be embarrassed, or proud?

Also, it's easy to forget that other people may be affected by the content of your message. For example, a friend may not appreciate the fact that you published a social communication with the information that her husband's out of town. You might feel comfortable putting information about yourself on a public forum, but other people may feel differently. Protect your own and others' privacy, including your co-workers, partners, and customers. If you want to mention an Intuit colleague on the Internet, get his or her permission first. Intuit's Privacy Policy prohibits the sharing of personally identifiable information.

We also must never disclose Intuit confidential information. Some examples of confidential information include anything related to Intuit financials, stock price, sales figures, business plans, future or unannounced products, features and release dates, inventions, strategy, processes, deals, and acquisitions that have not been made public. These rules might seem restrictive, especially when you want to correct someone else's inaccuracy or let a customer know about an upcoming feature. However, confidentiality rules protect our business, and stock price, and help us avoid serious regulatory issues. For more information about what Intuit considers to be confidential, see the related Overview. If you have a question about whether specific information about Intuit has been publicly disclosed, contact your manager or the Intuit Corporate Communications group. These rules also apply to third-party confidential information, including information about our partners and any personally identifiable information about our customers, partners, or employees.

In the casual atmospheres of social media and social communities, it can be easy to say something that could be interpreted by others as defamatory, obscene, embarrassing, or even harassing, threatening, libelous, or discriminatory. Remember that you can be held personally responsible for your comments, and your comments can expose Intuit to liability.

Never make negative comments about our customers, partners, suppliers or competitors. If you're not sure about how your comment might come across, run it by someone you trust and exercise your own good judgment. Err on the side of caution. After all, once your comments are out, you cannot take them back, and hundreds, if not thousands, of people may see them.

Also contact the Corporate Communications group if a financial analyst, member of the media, or blogger contacts you about an Intuit-related posting. You'll need help in responding to these potentially sensitive questions.

Good Example: Nancy has given me the okay to say that she loves living in Oakland . . .

Bad Example: Funny you should mention Nancy. She lives on Live Oak Street in Oakland and . . .

Good Example: Thank you for suggesting new feature ideas! I will be sure to pass them on!

Bad Example: You'll be happy to know that we're implementing that new feature in our next edition of QuickBooks Online! . . .

Good Example: Company financial information is outside of my expertise. I'd like to instead answer your question about how P3P works . . .

Bad Example: Intuit is financially healthy. You should definitely buy stock now . . .

## Guiding Principle: Spirited

### Policy:

■ Have fun and personify the value of spirited.

Finally, have fun! If you are excited about your job, your company, and your company's values, that's the way it should be. You should convey that excitement and represent Intuit's values in everything you do at work—including in your social communications.

# Additional Resources

One of the first things you'll realize as you start to immerse yourself in social media is there is no end to the number of blog posts, tweets, LinkedIn and Facebook groups, videos, podcasts, and conferences vying for your attention and claiming to be the one, definitive source for everything you need to know about enterprise social media.

(And once again, thank you for taking some of your valuable time to read this particular resource.)

Here's a more or less random collection of resources your authors have found useful, valuable, or enjoyable (and in some cases, all three).

## CONFERENCES AND INFORMATION PROVIDERS

Author Dave Thomas has spoken at several events put on by MarketingProfs, an organization that provides online resources, newsletters, and white papers and puts on excellent conferences. It does a great job sharing practical knowledge of how businesses are actually using social media. The panel discussion on B2B social media best practices at the May 2010 B2B forum in Boston was literally standing-room only.

Ragan Communications is another fine organization putting on practical and focused communications conferences, many of them centered on social media. Ragan often partners with major corporations to put on conferences at the company's facilities. Its events are well worth attending.

MarketingSherpa provides a wide variety of useful information as well. Both MarketingProfs and MarketingSherpa provide lots of useful information for free, and even more if you buy a membership.

## BLOGGERS AND FREE ONLINE RESOURCES

Some of the most useful social media case studies and best practices are handed out online for free. Insightful and knowledgeable social media speakers and consultants maintain excellent blogs where they share their ideas as well as information you can use right away.

Chris Brogan is president of New Marketing Labs. Chris's blog at www.chrisbrogan.com is perennially at or near the top of the AdAge Power 150 list of marketing bloggers (which in itself is a great resource for finding social media resources). Chris shares great ideas and information about social media for business. He also aggregates social media case studies at Delicious.com, the social bookmarking site. You can find it at http://delicious.com/chrisbrogan/casestudy. The team at New Marketing Labs also shares great stuff at http://newmarketinglabs.com/blog/.

David Armano is another well-known social media thought leader and senior vice president at Edelman Digital. His blog at http://darmano.typepad.com/ is called "Logic + Emotion," and that's a great description of David's approach. He's also a very visual thinker, and his blog is worth seeing just for the clear and clever ways he presents difficult concepts.

SocialmediaB2B.com is a blog started by Jeff Cohen and Kipp Bodnar. As they say in the United Kingdom, "It does exactly what is says on the tin." Jeff and Kipp have amassed an impressive collection of interviews and practical posts addressing all aspects of social media's role in marketing and community building in a business-to-business environment.

Marketing Over Coffee is a website (www.marketingovercoffee.com) and podcast run by Christopher S. Penn and John Wall. They do a great job covering the intersection of old and new marketing, skewed very heavily toward practical techniques designed to product measurable results. Plus they record it live in a Dunkin' Donuts outside Boston, which leads to a very convivial and enjoyable vibe, whether you've had your first cup of the day or not.

This is just a quick, short list to get you started. Dozens of other social media folks share practical information, including Justin Levy, Brian Solis, Jeremiah Owyang, Wayne Sutton, Charlene Li, Michael Brito, Jason Falls, Amber Naslund, DJ Waldow, CC Chapman, Mitch Joel, Mark Ragan, Ann Handley, Jason Keath, Katie Paine, and Keith Burtis. Once you start paying attention to a few of them, you'll naturally find yourself drawn to the others whom they reference and engage with.

By the way, the easiest way to follow online thought leaders like the ones listed is to set up a free RSS reader like Google Reader, which allows you to subscribe to blog feeds and scan through the headlines very quickly. In a few minutes a day you can read the information most relevant to you and quickly hone your list to the people from whom you get the most value.

The creation of Twitter lists allows you to quickly find groups of people worth following. If you find someone worth following in a topic that interests you, he or she may have created a list that interests you as well. For instance, Keith Burtis has created a list on his Twitter account (@KeithBurtis) called Analytics. He's grouped together people whom he follows to keep up with news about social media analytics. If you're interested in that topic as well, he's saved you a lot of time.

And of course if you start following the folks listed here on Twitter, you'll see the top social media news instantly and see what they're reading and sharing themselves. Many folks who use Twitter regularly find they end up getting most of their news—about social media marketing in particular and the world in general—from the people and organizations they follow.

## FREE ONLINE RESOURCES

Mashable.com is a great source for breaking social media news, often related to business, often not, but sometimes the news that isn't related to business at the moment will be related to business in a few weeks or months, if you know what we mean. For instance, a year ago, did you think your business would have to care about what Facebook was doing? Mashable gives a good look into the social media zeitgeist and a glimpse of where it's heading.

LinkedIn has become the de facto social network for business. (If you don't have a LinkedIn profile, you need to set one up now and go through the steps LinkedIn recommends to make it complete.) In addition to people connecting with you because they want to sell you something or work for your company, there are thousands of LinkedIn groups where people share their knowledge and expertise.

There are active social media marketing groups as well, and new ones starting every day. It's worth checking to see if there are LinkedIn groups devoted to marketing in your particular industry, as they can be an additional source of real-world information and best practices.

Facebook has many of the same types of groups that you'll find on LinkedIn, and it is increasing its focus on business every day. Once you've identified a list of groups worth following on LinkedIn, run some searches on Facebook to see if useful groups exist there too.

All of the channels mentioned require time and attention to read and follow, but the payoff can be high. Smart people are sharing practical information every day. Figure out how much time you can devote to learning more about enterprise social media—even if it's 20 minutes a day—and work to hone down the resources you follow to the ones you find most useful. In a few weeks you'll have a short, manageable, and valuable list.

# Recommended Reading

Barlow, Mike, and Michael Minelli. *Partnering with the CIO: The Future of IT Sales Seen Through the Eyes of Key Decision Makers*. Hoboken, NJ: John Wiley & Sons, 2008.

Benioff, Marc. *Behind the Cloud: The Untold Story of how salesforce.com Went from Idea to Billion-Dollar Company and Revolutionized an Industry*. San Francisco: Jossey-Bass, 2009.

Benkler, Yochai. *The Wealth of Networks: How Social Production Transforms Markets and Freedom*. New Haven, CT: Yale University Press, 2006.

Brogan, Chris. *Social Media 101: Tactics and Tips to Develop Your Business Online*. Hoboken, NJ: John Wiley & Sons, 2010.

Brogan, Chris, and Julien Smith. *Trust Agents: Using the Web to Build Influence, Improve Reputation, and Earn Trust*. Hoboken, NJ: John Wiley & Sons, 2009.

Collins, Jim. *Good to Great: Why Some Companies Make the Leap . . . and Others Don't*. New York: HarperBusiness, 2001.

Deming, W. Edwards. *The New Economy for Industry, Government, Education*. Cambridge, MA: MIT Center for Advanced Educational Services, 1994.

Downes, Larry. *The Laws of Disruption: Harnessing the New Forces that Govern Life and Business in the Digital Age*. New York: Basic Books, 2009.

Eiras, José Carlos. *The Practical CIO: A Common Sense Guide for Successful IT Leadership*. Hoboken, NJ: John Wiley & Sons, 2010.

Greenberg, Paul. *CRM at the Speed of Light: Social CRM Strategies, Tools, and Techniques for Engaging Your Customers*, 4th ed. New York: McGraw-Hill, 2009.

Greenleaf, Robert K. *Servant Leadership: A Journey into the Nature of Legitimate Power & Greatness*. New York: Paulist Press, originally published in 1977.

Juran, J. M. *Juran on Quality by Design: The New Steps for Planning Quality into Goods and Services*. New York: Free Press, 1992.

Katzenbach, Jon R., and Douglas K. Smith. *The Wisdom of Teams: Creating the High-Performance Organization*. Boston: Harvard Business School Press, 1993.

Kidder, Tracy. *The Soul of a New Machine*. New York: Little, Brown, 1981.

Kim, W. Chan, and Renee Mauborgne. *Blue Ocean Strategy: How to Create Uncontested Market Space and Make the Competition Irrelevant*. Boston: Harvard Business School Press, 2005.

Kotter, John P. *John P. Kotter on What Leaders Really Do*. Boston: Harvard Business School Press, 1999.

Kropotkin, Petr. *Mutual Aid: A Factor of Evolution*. London: William Heinemann, 1902.

Leistner, Frank. *Mastering Organizational Knowledge Flow: How to Make Knowledge Sharing Work*. Hoboken, NJ: John Wiley & Sons, 2010.

Levy, Justin R. *Facebook Marketing: Designing Your Next Marketing Campaign*. Indianapolis, IN: Que, 2010.

Li, Charlene. *Open Leadership: How Social Technology Can Transform the Way You Lead*. San Francisco: Jossey-Bass, 2010.

McAfee, Andrew. *Enterprise 2.0: New Collaborative Tools for Your Organization's Toughest Challenges*. Boston: Harvard Business Press, 2009.

Mirchandani, Vinnie. *The New Polymath: Profiles in Compound-Technology Innovations*. Hoboken, NJ: John Wiley & Sons, 2010.

Poundstone, William. *Priceless: The Myth of Fair Value (and How to Take Advantage of It)*. New York: Hill and Wang, 2010.

Ridley, Matt. *The Rational Optimist: How Prosperity Evolves*. New York: HarperCollins, 2010.

Rosenberg, Scott. *Dreaming in Code*. New York: Crown, 2007.

Scott, David Meerman. *The New Rules of Marketing and PR: How to Use Social Media, Blogs, News Releases, Online Video, & Viral Marketing to Reach Buyers Directly*. Hoboken, NJ: John Wiley & Sons, 2010.

Watkins, Michael. *The First 90 Days: Critical Strategies for New Leaders at All Levels*. Boston: Harvard Business School Press, 2003.

# About the Authors

**David B. Thomas** is Executive Director at New Marketing Labs, overseeing client relations. A marketing professional with more than 20 years experience in corporate and entrepreneurial environments, Dave came to NML from SAS, the leader in business analytics software and services. As Social Media Manager for SAS, Dave built on a global grass roots effort to create the company's social media strategy, policies, and training. Dave began his career in 1989 as a reporter and photographer for the *Chapel Hill News* in Chapel Hill, N.C. Before joining SAS he worked for Yep Roc Records, where he directed Web and social media marketing and launched the Web store. He has also held marketing and marketing communications positions at Nortel and Geomagic.

He has been actively engaging online since 1994 when he joined his first Internet forum, and began blogging in 2002 when he wrote the daily update for the Iceland Airwaves music festival. He lives in Carrboro, North Carolina with his wife, Jean, and his son, Conrad. You can learn more about Dave at dbthomas.com.

**Mike Barlow** is an award-winning journalist, author, ghostwriter, and communications strategist. Mike's 18-year career in daily newspaper journalism included stints at several respected suburban newspapers, including the *Times Herald-Record*, the *Journal News*, and the *Stamford Advocate*. His feature stories and columns have appeared in the *Los Angeles Times*, *Chicago Tribune*, *Miami Herald*, *Newsday*, *Hartford Courant*, and other major U.S. dailies. Mike lives in Fairfield, Connecticut, with his wife, Darlene, and their two children. He is coauthor of *Partnering with the CIO: The Future of IT Sales Seen Through the Eyes of Key Decision Makers* (John Wiley & Sons, 2007).

# Index